THE NEW SCOOP:

Recipes for Dairy-Free, Vegan Ice Cream in Unusual Flavors (Plus Some Old Favorites)

ALINA NIEMI

Alina's Pencil Publishing
2012

Find updates and corrections at www.alinaspencil.com

For more information, please contact the publisher at www.alinaspencil.com

ISBN: 978-1-937371-00-5
LCCN: 2011931882

DEDICATION

To the late Raymond Baker, who loved ice cream.

Sorry you never got to taste all these, man. I think you would have liked a lot of them.

Chocolate Raspberry Ice Cream

Contents

ACKNOWLEDGMENTS

This book would never have been possible without the help from all my testers, whose time, tongues, stomachs (and freezers!) came in so very handy.

Thanks to Dick and Eleanor Burson; Jonelle, Matt, Jacqueline and Melissa Oshiro; Jacqueline's friends; Myra, John and Jill Honjo; Glen Botha; Franklin Niemi; John Klopp; Paula Luv; George Segedin; Barbara Polk; and Sarah E. Hoffman.

Also thanks to my father, who didn't complain (too much) when all the freezers in the house were full of nothing but ice cream and frozen fruit. And to Percy, for making me laugh every day and loving every flavor I give him.

Thanks to Mashuri Waite at Lyon Arboretum, Honolulu, Hawaii, for his botanical knowledge.

Most of all, thanks to Joycee, for being my best guinea pig ever, for your discerning palate and total honesty, and for filling your freezer way past your comfort level. Your love and support mean the world to me, and I cherish you in my life. I love you so dearly. Thank you, Sweetie. I'll make you a batch of Blackberry Mint Sorbet and even strain the seeds out for you! (Or Mocha Almond Fudge, or Mint Chocolate Chip, or Mixed Berry Frozen Yogurt, or Taro Ice Cream, or...)

CHAPTER 1

The Inside Scoop (Who, What, Where, When, and Why of Making Ice Cream)

WHO can make non-dairy ice creams?

Anyone who has a desire to do so and the necessary equipment and ingredients. You might be looking to get away from eating dairy products for ethical or environmental reasons. Or you may be doing so for your health, or because you don't want animals to have to be used for milk, cream, butter and eggs.

Perhaps you have lactose intolerance or allergies, which make consuming dairy products uncomfortable or dangerous. You might not like the idea of consuming raw eggs in your frozen treats. Or maybe you just want to try something different.

In this book, you'll find recipes for ice cream, sherbet, sorbet, and frozen yogurt that are based on nondairy milks instead of regular milk. There are some with soy, and others with coconut, rice, or nut milks as bases.

You'll also learn how to make your own soy or coconut milk yogurt easily at home, then make frozen yogurt with them, at a fraction of the cost of what you'd pay to buy them already made. Better yet, you control what ingredients go into them, and you can make only the flavors you want.

Fruits get a starring role in some of the sorbets, which use no dairy-free milk products at all. Use fresh or frozen fruits, and for some of the tropical fruits, canned juices, fruits, or purees.

WHAT do you need to make homemade ice cream?

You need just a few pieces of basic kitchen equipment: measuring spoons and cups, blender, knife and cutting board, rubber spatulas, strainer, pots, containers for storage, and a freezer. To freeze the ice cream, you can use an ice cream machine, or just a container in the freezer and a fork (more on this later.)

You will also need ingredients, which will be covered shortly. You will need a sense of adventure, plus a little bit of patience.

I recommend having a pencil or pen for taking notes when you try these recipes. If you omit or add ingredients, change amounts, or alter the original recipe, it's a good idea to write that down.

Why? Because you are likely to forget what you did or how much you added. And if your new version comes out fantastic and you want to re-create it, you'll be able to make it again, easily, because you wrote it down the first time.

Trust me. Far too many times, I've not written something down, assuming I'll never eat it again, only to regret it later. Or added another spoonful of sweetener or vanilla, and then another, and then forgot how many I had added.

Save your time, energy, and money by writing it down the first time. And when you come up with your next flavor sensation, you'll have the recipe to prove you were the original creator.

WHERE can you make these frozen delights?

Anywhere you have access to preparation space and a freezer, or an ice cream machine that does not require a freezer. Some ice cream makers are free-standing, with their own compressor. You can make your ice cream in one of those machines and consume it immediately, without needing a freezer.

To be realistic, however, having a freezer works best, because most popular home ice cream machines use a canister that you must freeze before you can make your ice cream. And to store leftovers for later, or to make your finished products more firm, you will need to freeze them.

WHEN can you produce vegan ice creams, sorbets, and sherbets?

Whenever you want to! That's half the fun. Feel like a batch of Mocha Almond Fudge in the middle of winter? Go for it.

How about some refreshing Watermelon Sorbet or Cucumber Mint Frozen Yogurt in the midst of summer's heat? Not a problem.

Want to make Peanut Butter and Jelly Ice Cream with the kids on a rainy weekend? Wash your hands and dive in.

It is absolutely possible, under the right conditions, to have finished ice cream, sorbet, or sherbet in about 40 minutes, including mixing and freezing time. That's probably less time than it would take you to run to the store to buy some...if they're open, that is.

What are the right conditions? You need cold ingredients, or an already prepared and chilled base. Your freezer canister for your home ice cream machine needs to be fully frozen and ready to use, or you need to have a compressor-style ice cream maker.

In fact, if you already have your base mixed, chilled, and ready to go, you can be eating in as little as 15 to 20 minutes. Just pour your base into the ice cream machine and let it do its thing. How's that for getting your fix?

WHY make dairy-free, vegan frozen desserts?

Because you control everything that goes into it. The safety and quality of commercially prepared products is often less than ideal. Hormones and antibiotics are routinely given to farm animals in the United States to encourage faster growth, increased production, and reduced illness.

Where do those chemicals end up? In the milk, cream and eggs that go into commercial dairy-based ice creams and sherbets. And into your body.

Other questionable ingredients include food coloring. Have you ever seen a commercial orange sherbet that looked pale orange, like the milk and orange that it's made of, instead of artificial bright orange? I doubt it, because commercial manufacturers use chemical colors to make their products supposedly more appealing to the average consumer.

Maybe you're not an average consumer. I know I certainly don't feel good about eating something full of dyes that are labeled according to formula numbers, like Red Dye Number 36.

Pick up a package of commercial ice cream and read the label. It probably contains cream, milk, sugar, and likely includes corn syrup, some gum, and artificial coloring and/or flavoring. It may contain raw eggs, although, nowadays, due to the risk of contracting salmonella or other food-borne illnesses, they are uncommon.

It's likely you don't know what some of the ingredients on the label are. You might not be able to pronounce them. Why would you want to eat them?

For example, here is the ingredient list from a carton of Vanilla Ice Cream produced by a company whose website brags they make "real ice cream, from the finest and freshest of ingredients."

INGREDIENTS in Premium Vanilla Ice Cream: Milk, Cream, Sugar, Corn Syrup, Carob Bean Gum, Guar Gum, Mono & Diglycerides, Carrageenan, Vanilla Extract, Vanillin, Annatto (for color.)

Carrageenan is a seaweed, annatto is the seeds from a plant, and while they may be the finest and freshest, I don't particularly have any interest in eating guar gum or mono and diglycerides, whatever they are. I prefer to stick to things I know and trust, even if that means I won't be able to keep my ice cream scoopably soft for the next month. (Most gums and additives like carrageenan are to maintain soft, creamy texture over time.)

When you make your own ice cream, you know exactly what goes into it. You control what kind of fruit, sweetener, or flavoring you use. You control which ingredients go into your base mix. You are sure to leave out nuts if you are allergic to nuts. You don't add coconut milk if you don't like coconut milk. You add extra spice if you like it extra spicy.

YOU are the boss of your ice cream. When you make your own, you can experiment with different flavor combinations. You can try freezing your favorite kind of tea into a sorbet. You can use the herbs and vegetables from your garden. You can make up your own signature flavors.

I happen to hate green tea. I think it tastes like swamp water--not that I've ever tasted swamp water. But Green Tea Ice Cream is a popular flavor, and if you like green tea, you can try the recipe in this book and indulge until you're green.

Also, you can make varieties and flavors that you enjoy but might not be able to find in stores. Maybe you just love coffee and chai together, but nobody makes a Coffee Chai flavor. Make it yourself.

What if you love lychee, but the commercial stuff is just too sweet. Make your own and adjust it to your taste.

Maybe you go crazy with anticipation all spring and summer, waiting for pumpkin ice cream, but it's only sold during fall and winter. If you make it yourself, you can have pumpkin in May.

Finally, these nondairy frozen treats are lower in fat than their dairy counterparts. They have zero cholesterol. That's right, none, nada, zip, zilch, nothing. You can't say that about regular ice cream.

Yet they still have a creamy mouthfeel (or an icy one--you can control that, too) and all the flavor of commercial products. In fact, homemade in most cases tastes even better than store-bought.

It's like eating a tomato or a string bean that you've purchased from the grocery store, versus one you've grown yourself. It's the difference between picking a pea and eating it right off the vine in your back yard, versus from a bag of frozen peas, or even worse, from a can of mushy, olive-green lumps. Blech. No comparison.

After you've had Pear Sorbet (page 100), or Lemon Sherbet (page 99) made at home, from real fruits, you won't want to eat the commercial stuff anymore. At least, I'm guessing you won't.

Try it for yourself and see. You don't need a lot to get started. You don't even need an ice cream machine, although once you try a batch or two, you will love them so much, you'll run out and get a machine eventually, like I did.

In fact, I was making my own homemade, non-dairy, vegan ice creams, sherbets and sorbets for over 20 years before I tried an ice cream machine. I figured, how much difference could it make?

A lot! The consistency is much smoother and creamier without as much work on your part, especially if you get an electric ice cream machine. And you can have a finished product in a fraction of the time. So I highly recommend having one.

CHAPTER 2

Defining Frozen Delights

Tomato Basil Ice Cream

What's the difference between ice cream, sherbet, sorbet, and frozen yogurt? Here's a basic rundown.

Basically, frozen ice-cream-type mixtures can be divided up into three basic categories: ice creams, sherbets (or gelatos) and sorbets (or granitas.) The main difference is what kind of milk or milk substitute is used, or not.

ICE CREAM

According to the United States Food and Drug Administration, or FDA, which oversees production and regulation of commercial foodstuffs, commercial ice cream must contain at least 10% dairy fat by weight and 20% milk solids in order to be labeled as "ice cream" for sale.

Dairy fat, or butterfat, is the fat that is found in butter and cream from a cow. So by strict definition, there can be no such thing as a vegan or dairy-free ice cream. There are no milk solids or butterfat in vegan ice cream, since there is no milk, cream, or half and half.

But because there is no other widely accepted name, we will use the term "ice cream" to refer to any dairy-free, ice-cream-like, frozen concoction. We aren't concerned with fat percentages for our purposes, except to note that fat carries flavor.

In other words, if you want a richer, creamier dessert, you need to add more fat. Dairy ice creams use butterfat from cream, half and half, and milk. Eggs are often added as well, especially egg yolks, which contain fat and help to create a velvety texture.

Some traditional dairy ice cream recipes rely on raw eggs. Others use a cooked egg and milk custard, which is then frozen.

Vegan products use fats from nuts, seeds, legumes, and grains to replace the fats from the cows and chickens. Without fat, there would be very little flavor, and the mouthfeel would be more like water and less like cream.

To get an idea of the difference that fat makes, taste a pinch of cocoa powder, then taste a bit of chocolate bar. Cocoa powder has the fat (in the form of cocoa butter) removed. Chocolate still has the fat in it. Both taste chocolaty, but the bar chocolate has a decadent richness that is missing from the cocoa powder.

SHERBET

Commercial sherbets contain milk and fruit or other flavoring ingredients, such as chocolate or coffee. Vegan sherbets use coconut, soy, oat, almond, hemp, or rice milk instead of dairy milk.

Sherbets are lower in fat than ice creams, but they are also less creamy. However, because they still use nondairy milks, they have a creaminess to them that sorbets do not. So I like to think of them as kind of in between sorbets and ice creams.

Gelatos are frozen ice cream-like products originally from Italy, which use whole milk as the main dairy ingredient. They have a richer flavor than vegan sherbets, but the idea is similar.

SORBET

Sorbets are frozen fruits, juices, purees, or other liquids, such as herbal teas. The flavors can be quite intense and fruity and are often used as palate cleansers between courses during a fancy meal.

They have a higher proportion of water than sherbets and ice creams, so the consistency is much different. They can be icy, crunchy, or more slushy, depending on how they are frozen, but they will never have the rich creaminess of ice cream.

In fact, because they do not have that added fat, they are extremely healthy options for those who want to reduce their fat intake without sacrificing flavor or satisfaction. And their high water content makes sorbets extremely refreshing. A tangy, cooling fruit-mint sorbet will perk almost anyone up on a hot day.

GRANITA

Granitas are sorbet-like Italian frozen desserts that do not use an ice cream machine. They are supposed to have an icy, rougher texture. The base mixture is frozen in a pan in the freezer and scraped out with a fork. If you love icy frozen desserts, you can use this technique for your creations, including sherbets and ice creams.

There are no recipes for granitas per se in this book. But if you want that kind of icy finished product, simply freeze your base in a shallow, rectangular container. When you want to serve it, scrape some out with a fork or spoon. You may need to let it set out on a counter for a few minutes, to soften enough to do so.

FROZEN YOGURT

Frozen yogurts are made with yogurt instead of regular milk. In our case, we will be using soy or coconut milk yogurt. The tangy flavor of yogurt comes through in the finished product.

Frozen yogurt is also lower in fat and therefore less rich than ice cream. There is no added fat besides what is in the soymilk or coconut milk used to make the yogurt itself.

BASE + EXTRAS + FREEZING = FROZEN TREAT

The basic formula for all of the ice creams, sherbets, sorbets, and frozen yogurts are the same. You create a base mixture, add extra goodies, and freeze it all, although not necessarily in that order.

What kind of delicious things are we using? What makes vegan ice cream so creamy? The basics, plus the extra goodies, like nuts, chocolate, and fruit, are all discussed in the next chapter, Chapter Three: The Ingredients.

CHAPTER 3

The Ingredients

In order to make our ice creams, sherbets, and sorbets, we need a base mix and some extra goodies. Let's take a look at the ingredients we'll be using.

MILK SUBSTITUTES

The flavor and creamy richness in vegan ice creams comes, in large part, from nondairy milk products or milk substitutes. Because we are making egg- and dairy-free products, we need to replace the fat and milk-like flavor with other ingredients.

Any of these nondairy milks can be used interchangeably in the recipes in this book. However, if I have listed one specific type of milk first in a recipe, it means that one is preferred for that recipe.

Coconut Milk

Some nondairy ice cream recipes call for coconut milk. Because coconut milk has a high saturated fat content, it can mimic the creaminess and richness of milk.

The problem is that it has a pronounced flavor all its own. Many people do not like coconut milk and therefore don't want to use coconut milk-based recipes.

But if you don't mind the flavor, or enjoy the flavor, try some of the coconut-milk-based ice cream recipes in this book. Be sure to use full-fat coconut milk, not lite or reduced fat. If you're going to take all the fat out, you might as well give up, because the flavor and texture are substandard, and in my opinion, not worth the trouble.

Also, try to find coconut milk without added gums and starches, which tend to make an artificial-tasting, watery product. The ingredient list should just be coconut, water, and a preservative.

If you are using coconut milk that comes in a different size other than the cans I've used, one can of coconut milk is about 1-3/4 cups (437 milliliters) of liquid.

Soymilk

The next most common milk substitute is soymilk. This is made from blending soybeans and water, then adding salt, sweetener, and fat to create a product similar to cow's milk.

I used commercial soymilk in making the recipes in this book. If you opt to make your own soymilk, you may need to add some salt, sweetener, and fat to these recipes.

Every brand and style of commercial soymilk has different ingredients, flavor, and consistency. I recommend using a full-fat soymilk, not a reduced-fat type, and organic whenever possible. Otherwise, using either plain or vanilla soymilk doesn't seem to make a noticeable difference in the flavor of the finished products, so use what you like.

Try drinking a small amount before using it in one of the recipes. See if you find the taste of it enjoyable, or at least, palatable. If you are used to consuming dairy products, you might be disgusted when you first try soy and other milk alternatives.

But give it some time, and you'll get used to them. They will never taste like regular milk, obviously, but you can get a similarity that is close enough to work.

Some milks are a bit chalky, so try a couple different brands until you find one that works for you, or you can try making your own. Some people just don't enjoy the flavor of soymilk. In that case, try using almond or rice milk, both of which are commonly available these days in supermarkets and natural products stores.

Grain Milk

There are other types of milk substitutes on the market, including hemp milk, rice milk, and oat milk. They tend to be more watery and less rich-tasting than soymilks and coconut milk.

If you use these as your nondairy milk, you may want to add some fat to boost the flavor and texture to more closely mimic the higher-fat soy and coconut milks. Or you may like the lighter, cleaner flavor and texture.

Nut Milks

Nut milks, such as cashew and almond milk, are made by blending nuts with water, then straining out the nut solids. Because nuts are high in fat, they can be wonderful in nondairy ice creams and sherbets. Stay away from them if you have food allergies or sensitivities to nuts.

Another factor is cost. Nut milks are significantly more expensive than soy or rice milks, so some people may stay away from them for that reason. You can make your own nut milks (and grain milks) at home, although that may not reduce the cost by very much.

FATS

Fat carries flavor. So an ice cream, which has more fat, will taste richer and more fulfilling than a sherbet, which has less fat. Both of these will still be richer than sorbets, which have no added fat.

Some of the fat used in the ice creams in this book are those already contained in the milk substitutes. So I recommend using whole-fat varieties of whatever milk substitute you use, not reduced fat versions.

The other fats are added in the form of tofu, oil, or nut butters. Without these, you miss the creaminess and mouthfeel of an ice cream, even though you will get a smooth product.

Tofu

Tofu is basically coagulated soymilk, made from soybeans. It is used to give creaminess and body to the ice creams, giving them that certain "something" that makes them more satisfying.

You can use regular, water-packed, fresh tofu, but be sure to get it as fresh as possible and keep it refrigerated. Use it within a few days, because it can spoil quickly.

Some water-packed, fresh tofu now comes pasteurized, which means it has a longer shelf life. Check the expiration date and get something with the latest date possible, but the criteria for freshness apply to both pasteurized and non-pasteurized fresh tofu.

Fresh tofu has clear, not cloudy, water. It should have only a light fragrance, never a strong one, and should not be slimy or sour. If your tofu has slime on it or a sour flavor, it's too old. Dump it.

Aseptic boxes of silken tofu have an even longer shelf life and do not need to be refrigerated. Most people can find this in the Asian food aisle of their local grocery store, Asian markets, or Chinatown.

Whatever type of tofu you get, choose a medium or firm variety. You can use the very firm and soft varieties, but they are a bit more difficult to work with. If that's all you can get, however, use them. The main difference is the amount of water in each of them, which doesn't change the finished ice cream texture very much.

If you cannot or don't want to use soy, you won't be able to make any of the soy-based ice cream recipes in this book. However, you can still make the nut-based ice creams, coconut-milk-based ice creams, Avocado Ice Cream, and the sherbets and sorbets. Be sure to use a different type of milk in the sherbets, rather than soymilk. You can also make the frozen yogurts if you make your own coconut milk yogurt or use a commercial non-soy yogurt.

Oil

I use vegetable oil in the ice cream recipes. Along with the tofu, nut butters, and full-fat milks, it creates the texture that is the closest I can get to real dairy ice creams.

Any mildly flavored vegetable oil will do, such as sunflower, safflower, or light olive oil. Do not use extra virgin olive oil, which has a very strong flavor, unless you want that flavor in the finished product, because you will be able to taste it. I like canola oil, since studies have shown it to be healthy for the heart.

Soy Creamer

NONE of the recipes in this book call for soy creamer. Many other vegan ice cream recipes call for the use of soy creamer, a commercially made product. I do not like having to purchase so many commercially made products, especially not when they are so highly processed, as soy creamer is (and expensive!) Basically, it is made from soymilk, oil, and flavorings, plus starches, gums, and preservatives.

STARCHES

NONE of the recipes in this book call for added starches. Many other dairy-free ice cream recipes call for adding flour, tapioca starch, agar (a type of seaweed), arrowroot or cornstarch, to try to get better texture. But I find it unnecessary.

SWEETENERS

Most of these recipes use sugar or agave nectar. A few use maple syrup, dried fruits, or fruits for sweetener.

Sugar

Although you can use it in these recipes with fine results, white granulated sugar may not be a vegan product. In the refining process, the sugar is filtered through char, which can be made from vegetables or animal bones.

The only products used in this book that have white sugar in them are a few canned or pureed fruits, such as jackfruit, guava, lychee, and lilikoi (passion fruit), and the mango-pineapple juice used in the Tropical Sherbet recipe. You may be able to find these fruits fresh in your area, or find an unsweetened frozen source.

I use organic cane sugar, which is made from sugar cane, but not as highly refined as white granulated sugar. You can also use beet sugar if you have it available. There are also products labeled "dried sugar cane juice," which will work fine.

When using sugar as your sweetener, be sure to blend the base mixture long enough to dissolve the sugar. Some of the sugar products have larger crystals and take a little longer to dissolve than white sugar, or any liquid sweetener, would.

Sugar plays an important chemical role in the texture of the finished products, especially in sorbets, which have no fat. The sugar helps maintain a smooth texture. You can freeze pureed fruit without any sugar, but your sorbet will likely be hard and icy. Add some sugar, and your sorbet gets softer.

The trick comes in balancing sweetener for chemistry and sweetener for sweetness. Since many fruits are already naturally sweet, adding more sweetener would be overkill.

The workaround is to add water, tea, or other liquid, to dilute the sweetness, or to add something sour, such as lemon or lime juice, to help balance the flavors. Keep this in mind when you try making your own flavors.

Agave Nectar

People with blood sugar issues, like hypoglycemia or diabetes, will need to use something instead of sugar. Agave nectar, which is made from the cactus-like agave plant, keeps blood sugar stable, so it can usually be used safely by diabetics. Check with your doctor to be sure, before you try these recipes.

There are different brands and colors of agave nectar on the market these days. The lighter ones seem to have a lighter flavor, and the darker ones remind me of honey. The label on one brand recommends using only 3/4 of the amount of sugar called for in a recipe.

In other words, if the recipe calls for 1 cup (200g) of sugar, use 3/4 cup (188 ml) of agave nectar. However, in testing these recipes, I didn't need to make that adjustment. But keep that in mind if you decide to use agave nectar. You may need to adjust the amount, depending on the product you use.

Maple Syrup

Maple syrup, made by boiling the sap of maple trees, is delicious and naturally very sweet, but it is also very strongly flavored. I use it only in those recipes where the flavor will not clash with or overpower other ingredients. It is also very expensive, so I want to use it where I can taste it.

If you love the flavor and can afford to use it in place of the sugar or agave, by all means, go for it. You are the boss of your ice cream!

Stevia

Stevia is a plant or herb indigenous to South America. The leaves contain an ingredient that is 100 times sweeter than sugar. If you ever have the chance to pick a leaf of stevia and chew on it, you'll be amazed.

The problem is that if you just grind up the leaves and try to use them in place of sugar, it doesn't work. So most stevia on the market has had the sweet chemical extracted, and it is often blended with a fiber, to give it bulk.

You can try to use stevia extract in these recipes if you need to avoid sweeteners because of blood sugar issues, or if you need to limit your calories. Stevia has no calories and does not cause blood sugar to spike, like other sweeteners do (except agave nectar.)

But I haven't used stevia to test these recipes, and even if I had, I wouldn't be able to publish them, because there are so many stevia products out there, unless you use exactly the type of stevia I use, the recipe wouldn't work.

Stevia is so sweet, that even the tiniest amount more or less makes a huge difference in taste. Also, it can be bitter when you use too much, and some people seem to be more sensitive to that bitter flavor.

If you want to try to use stevia in these recipes, start by figuring out how much of your stevia product you would need to sweeten one cup (250 ml) of liquid. Most of these recipes contain between 3 and 4 cups (750 ml to 1 liter) of liquid, so add as much stevia as you would need for that much liquid.

Blend your base and taste it. It should be slightly sweeter than you want. Try freezing it and see how you like it. Write everything down, so you will be able to make your recipe again later if you want to, or adjust the ingredient amounts the next time.

Other sweeteners

Other sweeteners include fructose, brown rice syrup, barley malt syrup, date sugar, brown sugar, maple sugar, palm sugar, coconut sugar, and turbinado or raw sugar. These have not been tested in any of the recipes in this book, but don't let that stop you. If you want to try using them, follow the guidelines (above) for using stevia, and experiment with your sweetener of choice. Remember to write everything down, so you can refer to it later.

FRUITS

I have tried to use fresh fruits in season whenever possible for these recipes. Firstly because they just taste better, usually, than canned or frozen. Also because they are cheaper and fresher when they are in season than if they have been in a bag in your freezer for several months, and they have no added coloring or preservatives when fresh.

However, sometimes you can't get fresh fruits when you want them, in your area. So think ahead. I buy fruits in season and freeze them for use year-round.

Spring and summer are peak season for most fruits, including peaches, nectarines, berries, cherries, mangoes, and melons. Pears and apples are available in the fall and winter.

Try to buy fruits from local growers, to support your local farmers and businesses. And I always try to buy organic produce whenever possible, because it is healthier not only for everyone that eats it, but also for the farm workers and the environment as a whole.

Here are some guidelines for freezing fruit

Peel bananas. Freeze them whole or in halves.

Remove the skin and seeds from melons and mangoes. Cut them into smaller chunks.

Remove the seeds from papayas. Scoop out the pulp.

Remove the top from pineapples. Cut off the skin, eyes, and tough core. Cut the flesh into smaller chunks.

Remove the pits from plums, cherries, peaches, and nectarines. Leave cherries whole or cut them in half. Cut the other stone fruits into smaller pieces.

Remove the hulls from strawberries. Freeze small berries whole, and strawberries whole, halved, or sliced.

Place the fruits into air-tight containers or plastic bags and freeze them. I like to arrange them by fruit type so I can find them easily. I put melons on one shelf, berries on another, tropical fruits on another, and stone fruits on another.

You might also want to place a list on the door of your freezer. Write down the date and contents of each bag you put in there. That way, you can tell by looking at the list whether you have any more strawberries or should buy more while they are still in season. You can also tell when they were put in there and can use them up before the next season comes around.

When you use frozen fruits in your recipes, you may need to thaw them out slightly in order to measure them, or to prevent your blender from overworking and burning out. But you can also use this to your advantage. Frozen fruits in the base means a colder base, which means you get finished ice cream in even less time.

Fruit Zest

Some of the recipes call for the zest of fresh citrus fruits, like lemons and limes. I use a rasp-style zester to grate the zest. You can also use a vegetable peeler or knife to cut off thin slices of just the colored part of the zest. Don't use the white part just under the rind, because it's bitter. Then use a knife to finely chop the zest.

Always use organic fruits whenever possible if you are using the zest. Many of the chemical fungicides, pesticides, and herbicides that are sprayed on crops stay on the skins of fruits and vegetables. If you're going to eat orange peel, do you really want to consume whatever killing chemical cocktail might be on it as well? Consider paying a little more for organic produce now, rather than paying for it later with your health and well-being.

If you know someone who grows lemons in their yard and doesn't use any chemicals to grow them, you might make a trade. Ask them for lemons in return for a batch of homemade Lemon Sherbet. I don't know many people who would say no to that tasty offer.

Canned Fruits and Fruit Juices

Sometimes I use canned fruits and fruit juices. You may be able to find some of the juices in these recipes fresh, or make your own.

Feel free to substitute if you cannot get something. Try using prune juice if you cannot find pomegranate juice, for example. You won't get the same flavor, but you are likely to get a finished product that still tastes great.

HERBS

Most of these recipes use fresh herbs, because the flavor is brighter and sometimes altogether different from the dried. You can find fresh herbs sold in many grocery stores these days. Do not try to substitute dried herbs in these recipes.

If you want to experiment with herbs yourself, you have the option to blend the herbs into the ice cream base, or to steep them in the liquid, then strain them out and discard them. This is like making an herbal tea. It brings out more flavor, but it also means more time and effort in preparation. If you heat up your liquid to steep the herbs, you will need to cool it completely, then chill your base before you can churn your ice cream.

Mint, basil, thyme, lemony herbs (such as lemongrass, lemon verbena, lemon balm, and lemon basil), rosemary, anise hyssop, and lavender generally work well in sweets. But do not limit your mad kitchen science experiments to just those.

Try adding some tarragon or marjoram. If you're really adventurous, maybe some cilantro, oregano, or parsley? (I haven't used any of those yet, but you can blaze your own trail.)

Remember to take notes, so you can make them again if you like them, or adjust them if you need to. Or avoid them if you end up with disgusting combinations!

SALT

A small amount of salt is often added to increase flavor without adding more sugar or fat. You'd be surprised at how much of a flavor boost it creates, especially with some fruits.

Salt is essential in some of the flavors, such as chocolate, where it really brings out the chocolate-ness, and Toasted Almond Ice Cream and the Peanut Butter Ice Creams. Leaving salt out of those makes the flavors taste very flat and unappealing.

SPICES

I have used some dried spices, both in the whole and the ground form. The best place to find them reasonably priced and fresh are at a natural foods store, an Indian or Asian market, or Chinatown.

You may be able to find them in bulk and measure out exactly how much you want. Or you may find them already pre-bagged. Whichever form they are in, take a sniff before you buy.

Fresh spices, especially after they have been ground, will lose their fragrance as they get old. If the spices have no fragrance, or a very weak one, do not bother buying them. Yes, you should be able to smell them through the plastic bag, if they are bagged and fresh.

Ice creams made with spices will taste better after time, since flavors will infuse and meld to create a harmonious blend. Whenever possible, eat your ice creams with spices a day later, so they will taste even better than on the same day they were made.

NUTS

Nuts also show up in ice creams and sherbets in the form of butters and chopped nuts. Almond, peanut, and cashew butters, because they are high in fat, add creaminess and richness to ice creams.

If you are looking to eliminate the tofu from the ice cream recipes, feel free to play around with using nuts or nut butters instead.

Think about which nut would work best with the rest of the flavors, since most nut butters have strong flavors that will come through in the finished product.

Make sure you use fresh nuts. The oils can go rancid with too much time or heat, and will smell off. This also makes the nuts taste bitter and disgusting. Store your nuts in the refrigerator or freezer to prolong their life. Toasting them brings out more flavor.

To toast nuts

Place them in a dry pan on medium-high heat. Stir constantly and watch them closely, because they burn in a matter of seconds. They are done when they become fragrant and have a lightly browned exterior, which is hard to see, especially since many nuts are already brown to begin with. This normally takes about 7 minutes, but will vary depending on your stove and pan, so pay attention.

Remove them from the pan immediately and transfer to a container, so they do not continue to cook from the residual heat in the pan. If you want to use them right away, put them in the freezer to chill, so they don't raise the temperature of the finished ice cream or cause it to melt.

Nut Butters

Nut butters are high in fat and make very rich, thick ice creams. They have a strong flavor, so use them only when you want their flavor to come through.

Get an unsweetened natural product that contains just the nuts and sometimes some oil. Choose the creamy, not chunky, variety, since the chunks of nuts can get stuck in the blade of the ice cream machine, ruining your machine.

Some nut butters come in raw or roasted/toasted varieties. Roasted/toasted has a stronger, bolder flavor. Experiment to see what works for your purposes.

The oil and nut butter will probably have separated by the time you open the jar. Don't throw the oil away. Use a fork to carefully stir the oil back in, until you have a smooth, creamy product. This may take a fair amount of time. Store the jar in the refrigerator, all mixed, so it stays that way, and you won't have to mix it again.

CHOCOLATE AND COCOA POWDER

When using cocoa powder, use unsweetened. You will be able to make ice cream fairly quickly, provided the other ingredients are already chilled. The tradeoff is that you don't get as rich a flavor or texture as you do when you use full-fat chocolate, because cocoa powder has had the fat removed from it.

When using chocolate, use semi-sweet chocolate chips or any chocolate bar (make sure it does not contain milk) of your choosing. I tend to alternate, depending on the recipe. I like dark chocolate in Mint Chocolate Chip Ice Cream and Raspberry Chocolate Chip Frozen Yogurt. But I prefer semi-sweet chocolate for the swirl in Vanilla Bean Chocolate Swirl Ice Cream and cocoa powder for the fudge in Mocha Almond Fudge Ice Cream.

And in case you're wondering what the difference is between fudge, marble, ripple and swirl, there is none. I've used different names just for variety. Kind of like calling green beans by the French name, *haricots verts*. Sounds more delicious somehow, doesn't it?

I have included two chocolate ripple/fudge/swirl/marble recipes in this book: Fudge Ripple or Marble Sauce #1; and Fudge Ripple or Marble Sauce #2.

One of them uses chocolate chips or bar chocolate; the other uses cocoa powder. Both can be used interchangeably in any of the ice creams that call for them, such as Mocha Almond Fudge, Almond Coconut Ice Cream, Bumpy Road, or Vanilla Bean Chocolate Swirl Ice Cream. (See more information below.)

I keep my chocolate bars in the refrigerator. It helps them to last longer, prevents melting, and keeps the bugs out, especially important in the tropical climate where I live. It also helps to make them easier to chop.

To easily chop chocolate bars, use chilled chocolate. Then slice along the edges with a sharp knife. The chocolate will be brittle and break off in small shards and shavings, which makes them easier to melt.

Chocolate Chips

See Other Goodies, below.

ALCOHOL

By alcohol, I mean beer, wine, spirits and liqueurs. None are used in this book. If you want to experiment with them, feel free. However, there are a few things you need to know before you do.

First, alcohol affects the freezing of the ice cream. Your base will take longer to freeze. If you add too much alcohol, the mixture will not freeze at all.

Second, it softens the finished product. That can be a good thing if you are making sorbets, for example, which tend to freeze rock hard, especially once you transfer them to your freezer. But it also means softer ice creams, which might not be quite so welcome.

So keep that in mind if you want to try adding alcohol to any of the recipes. Write down what you do, so that you can duplicate or change it the next time.

One final suggestion: don't bother trying to add rum to the Lychee No-jito Sherbet. Some friends tried it and all agreed that it's better without it.

COFFEE

The coffee used in these recipes is in the form of instant coffee powder. You can use decaffeinated or regular coffee and alter the strength to suit your taste. Be sure to dissolve the powder in a small amount of hot water before adding it to your base.

FLAVORED WATERS

A handful of recipes in this book use flavored waters. They add more aroma than taste, but they are so unique, there really is no substitute for them.

Find them in Middle Eastern or possibly Asian or Indian grocery stores. You might also find them in the ethnic aisle of your supermarket, if there is a large Middle Eastern population, or in a natural products store.

Rosewater

Rosewater is made by steaming rose petals. The result is a clear, perfume-like water with a delicate flavor. Try experimenting by adding this to other flavors.

Orange Blossom Water

If you've smelled the flowers from any citrus tree, or from a mock orange bush, you have an idea of the sweet, alluring fragrance of orange blossom water. Use a light hand, as this can get sickly sweet.

VANILLA

I use vanilla extract in many of the recipes to give more depth of flavor. Use a good quality, real vanilla extract, because the flavor really comes through in the finished product.

Some recipes, such as those with lemon, will taste absolutely flat without the vanilla, so I don't suggest leaving it out. If the flavor seems too strong for you, reduce the amount slightly.

For the Vanilla Bean Ice Cream, you'll need to use a whole vanilla bean. They are sold dried and are fairly expensive. Spice stores, gourmet food stores, or online, will have them cheaper in bulk.

The flavor you get when you use vanilla bean is so much better than with vanilla extract. If you can afford it, definitely give the Vanilla Bean Ice Cream recipe a try. It's well worth the money spent.

VEGETABLES

I won't debate whether they are botanically fruits or vegetables. In these recipes, I consider tomatoes, corn, pumpkin, cucumber, carrots, sweet potatoes, beans and taro as vegetables. They are used in various forms--fresh, canned, or frozen.

I hope you try some of the recipes with vegetables in them, even if they sound horrible to you. Azuki Bean Ice Cream has become a favorite of mine, even though I've never really liked azuki beans per se. And Taro Ice Cream was a tester favorite, oddly enough, because I was going to throw the whole batch out when I first made and tasted it.

So don't be too quick to cross the unusual vegetable ice creams off your to-try list. Besides, if you never try them, how will you know one of them won't be the best thing you've ever had?

OTHER GOODIES, Also known as Mix-Ins

Mix-Ins are those things like crumbs, nuts, fruit pieces, coconut-- anything that is not completely smooth. Save your mix-ins for the end of the freezing process. If you add them earlier, they may scratch your machine and ruin your mixing paddle, which would be a very bad thing.

If you are using an ice cream machine, add them once the base has frozen to a soft-serve consistency. Then run the machine an additional 2 to 5 minutes, for the ice cream to finish firming up.

I like to stop the machine, take the mixing blade out, and stir my mix-ins by hand. Then I place the finished product into the freezer in an airtight container and let it finish firming up for another several hours. I just like getting more involved in the process and don't mind waiting to eat my ice cream.

Adding mix-ins late also means they will stay intact and not get broken up too much. For that reason, if you don't have an ice cream machine, wait until your mixture is almost completely frozen before stirring in your mix-ins.

Return the mixture to the freezer to finish firming up completely. This usually takes an additional 2 hours or more, depending on your freezer and the container you are using. You can speed up this process by putting your ice cream into several smaller or shallower containers, which will freeze more quickly than large or deep ones.

Fruit pieces

Feel free to add chunks of fruit as mix-ins at the end of the freezing process. Keep in mind that because they have a very high water content, some fruits will turn into icy chunks.

But you might like that combination of creamy ice cream with icy frozen bits. I have a friend who loves that, so whenever I make strawberry ice cream for her, I stir in strawberry bits at the end.

Crushed baked goods

One old-fashioned flavor of ice cream goes back to the Victorian era, when ice cream was only for the rich (find out why in the next chapter.) Brown Bread Ice Cream was made by mixing in crumbs from stale loaves of whole-grain bread.

You can use this as inspiration and add crumbs or chunks of other baked goods. Brownies, gingersnaps, snickerdoodles, cake, speculoos, and the ever-popular chocolate cookies or sandwich cookies are all delicious additions.

Pretzels are also nice. Be aware that many of these baked add-ins may get soggy over time, so if you want to make sure you get the crunchy texture, eat the ice cream the same day you make it.

Coconut

I use only unsweetened, shredded coconut in all the recipes. You may need to go to a natural foods store to get it unsweetened.

Sometimes I add it just as it is, and other times I toast it, which changes the flavor. It depends on what I am going for in the recipe.

TO TOAST COCONUT

Place unsweetened, shredded coconut in a dry pan over medium heat. Stir constantly until the mixture changes color, usually after about 7 to 10 minutes. Watch carefully once it starts to get fragrant, because it can go from perfect to burned in a matter of seconds.

Toast it just until it has turned light brown. Do not continue to a rich brown, or the flavor will be too overpowering.

If you do toast it too much, beyond the light brown stage, don't throw it out. Use it in Malaysian curries with coconut milk, where the strong toasting adds a distinct flavor to dishes such as vegetarian *rendang*, a dry curry originally from Indonesia.

Chocolate chips

Most homemade ice cream books tell you to dump in some commercially made chocolate chips as mix-ins. But I'll let you in on the secret way that ice cream producers make their chocolate chips.

They melt chocolate and add oil to it. Then they drizzle the mixture in at the end of the freezing process. When the chocolate hits the frozen ice cream, it immediately hardens.

The continuous churning of the mixture breaks up the chocolate into smaller shards, chips and chunks. For best results, add the chocolate in a small, steady stream, to prevent huge gobs of solid chocolate clumps from forming (unless, of course, you like that.)

TO MAKE CHOCOLATE CHIPS

Follow the directions in Mint Chocolate Chip Ice Cream or Raspberry Chocolate Chip Frozen Yogurt. You can use either dark chocolate, chocolate bars, or semi-sweet chocolate chips, whichever you prefer.

NOTE: You cannot use this method unless you have an ice cream machine. If you are freezing without one, substitute commercial chocolate chips instead, and stir them in, like you would any other mix-in ingredient, toward the end of the freezing process.

Chocolate Fudge, Marble, Ripple, and Swirl

This is a melted chocolate mixture or chocolate sauce which is layered among the frozen ice cream and sometimes swirled slightly. The whole thing is then placed in the freezer to harden completely.

The marbling or swirling is only apparent when the ice cream is scooped. Otherwise, it's just puddles and gobs of chocolate lying randomly in the ice cream.

To make chocolate fudge, marble, ripple, or swirl, follow the directions in the Mocha Almond Fudge Ice Cream recipe, in Chapter Seven (page 67.) You can add a fudge ripple to any flavor you like. Again, be the boss of your ice cream and make it how you like it.

Now that you know what ingredients you will need, the next step is to have the right tools for the job. For that, we move to Chapter Four: The Equipment.

Almond Coconut Ice Cream

CHAPTER 4

The Equipment

Even if you don't have an ice cream machine already, you probably have all the tools you need to make ice cream at home, right now. They are basic pieces of equipment, such as measuring spoons, a whisk, a blender, and pots. You'll also need some airtight containers to store the ice cream in the freezer after it has churned.

But I highly recommend getting an ice cream machine. The time it saves you is enormous, and the texture is much better than doing it by hand. You will learn why in the next chapter. For now, here is a brief rundown on a few tools of the trade, including the different types of ice cream machines.

Spatula

I recommend a flat-edged, silicone spatula. I have one with a sturdy bamboo handle. The silicone means it will stand up to the cold (or hot) temperatures without breaking down or melting.

The blade is not rounded at the corners, like most spatulas on the market. Instead, it has a rectangular corner and a thin, flat, rigid edge. It's not very flexible, like most others are.

This spatula is ideal for making ice creams, because not only will it scrape out the blender after I am done mixing the base, but it is perfect to scrape out the ice cream machine canister. The ice cream base freezes first where it touches the cold canister.

When you remove the ice cream to another container for storage, whatever is stuck to the sides of the canister gets even firmer. The flat, thin blade of the spatula helps to scrape all of it off, without scratching the walls.

Make sure to use something that won't scratch the walls of your ice cream machine. You need to take care of it so it will keep working properly for you, and you can rely on it when you have those sudden ice cream cravings.

Blender

You'll need a blender to make most of these recipes, especially the ice creams and anything with fruits in it. You can get away with just whisking many of the bases, but for those with fruits or tofu, you need to blend them to get the ingredients well mixed.

You cannot use a food processor, because the liquid will spill out the hole at the bottom. If you don't have a blender, you can get one very cheaply at a second-hand or thrift store.

A glass container works better than plastic. I also prefer them to stainless steel, because the clear glass means you can watch the blending to see that things are not sticking to the sides and are blending well. And unlike plastic, glass will not hold odors and get stained from colored foods like tomatoes, berries, and spices.

Storage Containers

You will need airtight containers to store your treats in the freezer. The high fat content of ice cream means that off flavors are more likely to be absorbed from your freezer if you don't cover them. On the other hand, you will probably eat them before they have a chance to absorb freezer odors.

I use plastic containers and prefer using several smaller ones to one larger one, to store each batch. Smaller containers freeze faster. They are also easier to find space for in the freezer, and I can take out one container and have it all for dessert, rather than scooping from a larger container.

Most plastics get brittle when frozen. And our freezers are always quite full of stuff, which means lots of containers end up falling out when we open the freezer door. You will likely lose containers, since they tend to shatter when they hit the ground.

An easy solution is to ask friends and neighbors to save appropriate sized containers for you. You will save yourself money by not having to buy containers, and you will be reducing the amount that is thrown away. An added bonus is the fact that many of the covers will fit on other bases. So when you break something, you will likely be able to find a matching, intact replacement to use.

My favorite containers are shallow, such as smaller tubs from margarine or sour cream, or rectangular containers from luncheon meat. You can also use larger tubs from non-dairy whipped topping or yogurt, cottage cheese, and the like. Those larger containers will usually hold one finished batch of ice cream, or one batch of homemade yogurt.

My friends and neighbors are more than happy to give me their unwanted containers. Of course, I supply them with a batch of some frozen delight every now and then, too, to keep them happy.

Ice Cream Machine

The final, and most important piece of equipment is your ice cream maker. Although it is not necessary to use one to make ice cream, I highly recommend getting one. The texture is much better, and if you get an electric model, it does all the work for you.

Also, the time it takes to churn a batch is reduced dramatically. You can make a batch in your freezer, without an ice cream machine, and it will take about 6 to 8 hours to finish freezing.

On the other hand, with an ice cream machine, that time can be cut down to about 30 minutes or less. If you want to do some work, you can opt for a hand-cranked machine and get a workout, plus the benefit of smoother texture and faster freezing time.

All the recipes in this book will fit in a 1-1/2 quart ice cream machine. The style of machine doesn't matter.

Here is a rundown of the basic types of ice cream machines.

Hand-Cranked Ice Chest

Back in the Victorian era, ice cream machines were basically buckets with a crank, set into larger buckets filled with ice and salt. The ice was expensive and hard to get. Most ice was cut from frozen lakes in the Northeastern part of the United States and shipped all over the world.

The ice had to be crushed and mixed with rock salt, to lower the temperature, so that the ice cream base would freeze. The base was placed in a smaller bucket with a handle, and someone--usually a servant--got stuck with the exhausting job of turning that handle until the ice cream was frozen.

The melting ice/salt mixture often spilled over into the ice cream. Salty, watery ice cream was no fun. Because of all the work and expense, ice cream was a treat savored by only the very rich, or by those who had connections.

Nowadays, you can still use the old-fashioned ice and salt bucket method. Some people enjoy the anticipation of waiting for your ice cream, and working for it. You might decide to hand-crank your ice cream to offset some of the calories you will ingest when you eat it. Or you may opt for this low-tech method when you go camping.

There are still bucket-style ice cream machines for sale that require the use of ice and salt. There are also machines that are made to look like the old buckets. They don't need ice and salt (they use a frozen gel canister), but you still need to do the cranking by hand. And then there are those machines that look more modern, use a frozen gel canister, so you can skip the ice and salt, but still make you crank.

Frozen Gel Canister Machines

The most affordable yet efficient ice cream makers use a canister filled with a special gel that freezes colder than water. You need to completely freeze that canister in your freezer before attempting to make a batch of ice cream.

They come in both manual and electric models. Manual models make you do the work. Electric models do the churning for you.

When you want to make a batch of ice cream, you take the canister out of the freezer, assemble your machine, and add your ice cream base. Then the machine needs to crank continuously for the 30 minutes or so it takes to freeze the base into semi-solid ice cream.

Churning it manually can be a fun activity if you have kids. Be forewarned, however, that their arms are likely to tire out after about two minutes, which means you will probably end up finishing the work. Of course, when the ice cream is done, everyone else's arms will be well rested and ready to shovel spoon to mouth, while yours may feel like they are ready to fall off.

Electric machines, on the other hand, churn the ice cream using a motor. That leaves you time to prepare your mix-ins or toppings, get containers ready, and spoons to eat with.

I love my electric machine. I take the frozen canister out of the freezer, assemble the machine, plug it in, turn it on, add my base, and have finished ice cream in about 15 to 30 minutes. There is some noise, but it sounds about as loud as an electric can opener. Not bad, considering what it does.

You can find out what machine I recommend, and read a review of it at my blog: http://www.almostveganinparadise.com

Itty Bitty Freezer-Type Machines

The top-of-the-line of ice cream machines are those that have a compressor and motor built in. They work like your normal-sized freezers, with churning ability added.

You plug the machine in and turn it on, and the machine provides the coolant to freeze your ice cream, without you needing to keep a canister in your freezer. Of course, the price you pay for this great convenience is quite steep.

Compare a gel-canister, electric model, which can easily be had for less than $100 U.S. and often under $50. On the other hand, these powerful freezer-type machines cost between $300 U.S. to $1000 or more.

Whether you choose to churn by hand or not, you will be rewarded with delicious, healthier, home-made ice creams. There's only one more thing to understand before you can begin your first batch-- good technique. That's next, in Chapter Five. Knowing this ensures you get the texture you want, so read on...

CHAPTER 5

How to Freeze Your Stuff

You don't need an ice cream machine to make any of the recipes in this book, although I highly recommend using one. To make ice cream, you will make a base. Then, you have two options: 1) Use an ice cream machine to freeze and churn, or 2) Do the work yourself, mixing multiple times during the freezing process. Let's compare these two options.

What are the benefits of using an ice cream maker?

Texture and Time

The main benefit is texture. When the ice cream base freezes, ice crystals form in the mixture. The longer it takes to freeze, the larger the ice crystals. Ice crystals make the ice cream crunchy and icy. If you like that, there is no need to invest in an ice cream machine.

But most people want a smooth, creamy texture. An ice cream maker breaks up the ice crystals as soon as they form, so that they are too small for your tongue to feel, and it freezes the base more quickly, reducing crystal formation.

Time is also a factor. Freezing by hand takes up to 8 hours. Using a machine reduces that to as little as 15 minutes.

Your labor

If you get a hand-cranked ice cream machine, you will need to turn the handle to churn the mixture as it freezes. An electric machine will do everything for you.

The other option is to freeze it yourself, without an ice cream machine. Here is how to do that.

How to make ice cream without an ice cream machine

If you like a crunchy, icy texture, freeze your base in a covered container in the freezer. That's it. You're done. Wait until the ice cream has frozen, then eat it.

However, if you want a smoother, less icy texture, you must break up the ice crystals as they form during the freezing process. You'll be doing the work that the paddle does in an ice cream machine.

There are three options for breaking up the crystals:

Option One

Prepare your base. Place it in a container in the freezer.

Every 30 to 60 minutes, use a fork to stir the mixture vigorously, breaking up the ice crystals. You'll find more crystals along the edges of the container.

Repeat over several hours, or until you don't feel that much of a difference between stirrings.

Stir in any mix-ins if you are using them. Place the mixture in an airtight container (if it's not already in one.) Freeze it several more hours, until firm enough to eat. The total time involved takes about 6 to 8 hours.

Option Two

Prepare your base. Place it in a container in the freezer.

After 2 or 3 hours, use a fork to break up the crystals that have formed along the edges. Stir the mixture vigorously. If the mixture is very liquid, and you are using mix-ins, come back in a few hours, when the mixture has reached a somewhat firm consistency.

Add your mix-ins at that time, and stir to mix. Return the mixture to the freezer in an airtight container for several more hours, until firm enough to serve.

If you are not using mix-ins, after you've broken up the ice crystals with a fork, freeze the mixture in an airtight container for several more hours, usually at least 6 more, until firm enough to serve.

Option Three

Prepare your base. Place it in a container in the freezer.

After 3 or 4 hours, or when the mixture has frozen halfway to the center of the container, dump the mixture into a blender. Blend for only a few seconds, to create a slushy or milkshake consistency. If the mixture is very thick, you may need to stop the blender and push lumps down with a spatula.

Return to the freezer in an airtight container to finish freezing, or until firm enough to serve, usually for another 6 hours or more.

With any of these three options, you are responsible for breaking up ice crystals. If you simply freeze the mixture without doing this, you will get a crunchy product with layers of large ice crystals which overlap like shingles on a roof.

How to make ice cream using an ice cream machine

Prepare your base

Make your base as directed in the recipe. Have your mix-ins standing by. If the recipe calls for chocolate swirl or marble, be sure it is cooling or already chilled while you churn your ice cream.

Always follow the manufacturer's directions with your ice cream machine. The following guidelines will work for most gel-canister, electric models.

Chill your base (or use chilled ingredients)

Make sure your ice cream base is chilled. This could take several hours, or you could leave it in the refrigerator overnight.

Alternately, keep your raw ingredients chilled, so when you make the base, it is already cold. Keeping ingredients in the refrigerator or freezer means you can whip up a batch on a whim, from start to finish, in about 40 minutes. (Read more in the next chapter.)

Freeze your canister

Make sure your canister is completely frozen. This could take from 8 to 24 hours. If you hear sloshing when you shake it, it needs to be frozen longer.

If you have a machine with a built-in compressor, you don't need to worry about this step. You are free to make ice cream at any time.

Assemble your machine

Take the frozen canister out of the freezer and assemble your ice cream machine. Turn it on.

Add your chilled ice cream base.

Let your machine do its work

At first, the mixture will just swirl around with the movement of the canister. Then you will begin to see some of the mixture that has frozen and been scraped off the sides. It will collect on the mixing paddle blade.

After about 5 more minutes, the mixture will have thickened and started to form mounds. If you dip a finger in at this time, it will be very soft and slushy and will drip off your finger immediately.

After another 5 minutes or so, the mixture will be getting firmer. Now if you dip a finger in, you will be able to hold the ice cream on the tip of your finger if you curve it so it doesn't fall off. You're more than halfway done.

Approximately 5 minutes later, the mixture will be a soft-serve consistency. The mounds will be firmer and the ice cream will hold its shape on your finger without you bending it.

It will take between 15 and 25 minutes for the mixture to reach this soft-serve consistency.

Add your mix ins

Now is the time to add your mix-ins.

If you are making chocolate chips, drizzle the melted chocolate in a small, steady stream. If you are using other mix-ins, dump them in.

Let the machine run another 2 to 5 minutes, to firm up.

Alternately, you can stop the machine, remove the mixing paddle, and stir in your mix-ins by hand. Then place the ice cream into containers in the freezer to harden, which takes several more hours.

If you are using a chocolate marble/swirl/ fudge/ripple, stop the machine and remove the paddle. Layer the ice cream into a container and add blobs of the chocolate mixture between layers. Place the container in the freezer for several hours to firm up. (Find complete instructions in the Mocha Almond Fudge Ice Cream recipe, in Chapter Seven, page 67.)

After You've Frozen Your Ice Cream

Oh yes, there's even more to learn...

Overrun and what it means for you

Commercial products get their creamy, scoopable texture from additives, such as gums and starches. Overrun, which is the addition of air into the mixture during the freezing process, also helps to keep ice cream soft. Frozen air is easier to scoop than frozen liquid or fruit.

By law, commercial ice cream in the United States is allowed to have 100% overrun, or half air. Think of how much you are paying for up to one half a container of air when you buy commercial products...

Homemade ice creams do not have as much air incorporated. As a result, the flavor is more intense. The downside to this is that the finished products freeze rock hard, or stay scoopable for only a short while in your freezer, so you need to make a few adjustments.

The sweet window for optimal taste and texture

It's recommended that you eat your finished products within a few hours to days after churning. Some mix-ins, like the pretzels in Chocolate Pretzel Ice Cream, get soggy quickly, so they are best enjoyed the same day they are mixed. Some recipes get extremely hard and become difficult to eat.

Realistically speaking, however, most people probably won't consume an entire batch of ice cream at one sitting. So if you freeze it and eat it later, you may need to temper the finished product.

What's tempering?

Tempering is warming the ice cream slightly, so that it melts a little and softens enough so you can scoop it. This can be done in two ways.

Countertop Tempering

Remove the frozen product before you plan to serve it. Place it on your countertop and allow it to sit at room temperature from 5 to 20 minutes, depending on the mixture. This will vary depending on the recipe you use, how warm it is, and how much is in the container.

Some recipes tend to melt very quickly. Sorbets made from only juices or teas can be especially tricky, since they freeze rock hard but tend to melt into liquid, rather than smooth sorbet. Ice creams usually take a little longer--usually about 15 or 20 minutes.

Microwave Tempering

Remove the frozen product. Take off the lid. Place in the microwave for just a few seconds on high power. I usually do about 10-15 seconds for a half-recipe-sized amount. Be very careful with this, because a few seconds will cause everything to melt, and if you just throw it back into the freezer again, you'll get ice crystals, not smooth ice cream.

So the safer bet is countertop tempering, if you have the patience for it. If I am having a dinner party and want to serve ice cream with dessert, I take it out when we start our entrée course. By the time we have finished, the ice cream is soft enough to serve and is starting to melt.

Of course, this won't work if your guests are very chatty and eat slowly, because you'll end up serving them puddles. In that case, wait until everyone is done eating, then take the ice cream out, and encourage another 5 to15 minutes of conversation before serving it.

Homemade Ice Cream Shelf Life

Your homemade vegan ice cream will not last as long in the freezer as commercial products will. Sorbets, especially those made with lots of liquid, can become like blocks of ice, and even tempering won't allow you to scoop them easily. Ice creams will be harder to scoop and will get very hard when frozen, especially as time goes by. After several weeks, tiny ice crystals will form on the surface.

For these reasons, it's recommended you consume your frozen treats within about 3 weeks after making them.

On the other hand, it's hard to imagine they will stay around for that long. When you make your own, you make flavors you love, and you can adjust each recipe until it's exactly as you like it. The finished products end up tasting so good, you almost cannot stop yourself from eating them.

As one of my testers commented:

> "I took a bite and it was interesting. The flavors were intense and not something I expected to find in my ice cream. Then I took another bite, and another, and I couldn't stop eating it. Before I knew it, I had eaten it all. So I guess that's a 'yes' for that flavor."

Before you make your first batch, check out the tips next, in Chapter Six: Getting Your Fix, or Tips For Making Ice Cream Fast. They will help you when you have a craving and want ice cream NOW, not tomorrow.

CHAPTER 6

Getting Your Fix, or Tips for Making Ice Cream Fast

I know one of the reasons you are looking at this book is because you want to eat ice cream at the spur of the moment, when you feel like it, without waiting overnight for a base to chill. Is that possible?

Yes, it sure is, in most cases. There are some recipes that you cannot make quickly, because the base needs to be heated first in order to infuse flavors or melt chocolate.

But most of the recipes in this book can be made within about 40 minutes, start to finish. You will need to do some advance preparation, so that when the mood strikes, you can forge ahead and churn, baby, churn.

Here is what you need to do.

Keep your ingredients cold

Fresh tofu must be refrigerated anyway, but put your aseptic box of tofu in the fridge too, so it's ready to go whenever you are.

Keep your milks chilled. I keep boxes of nondairy milk in the fridge at all times. If I have less than half a box remaining, I chill another box too, since I know I use about half a box per recipe.

Keep one or two cans of coconut milk in the fridge. This will solidify the coconut oil, causing it to clump into a solid mass of coconut cream at the top of the can. Before you open the can, shake it very well, to break up the lumps.

Keep your nut butters chilled. This keeps them mixed, preventing the oils from separating. That way you don't have to re-stir them when you want to use them. Also, they won't raise the temperature of your base when you make it.

Keep your fruits in the refrigerator or freezer. You can usually throw them into your base while they are still frozen. They will chill the base even more. When you go to churn, you'll get ice cream in even less time. This works well with recipes with lots of other liquid ingredients.

This may not work if you have a lot of fruits in a particular recipe, because it will be too thick to blend easily. In that case, thaw them slightly, so that you can easily measure and blend them without overtaxing your blender.

No need to refrigerate your sweetener or oil. If you keep the other ingredients chilled, that is enough to make the base cold enough to churn quickly.

Make sure your canister is completely frozen

If you shake it and hear gurgling, it needs to be in the freezer for a longer period of time.

Start churning immediately after you take your canister out of the freezer

The gel starts to warm up right away, and if you wait too long, you are losing its chilling potential. Grab your base and your machine and move quickly.

Use cocoa powder instead of chocolate if you want to make a chocolate flavor

You have the option of using either cocoa powder or melted chocolate in the chocolate ice cream recipes. Using cocoa powder means you can churn immediately. Melting chocolate means hours of chilling the base before you can churn.

You sacrifice a bit of richness in texture and flavor when you use cocoa powder. But if you want that chocolate fix right away, that may be an adequate tradeoff.

If you follow these simple steps, you can measure and mix your base in about ten minutes, then proceed immediately to churning. In another 15 to 20 minutes, you can have finished ice cream.

Okay, you've learned everything you need to know. You can jump to Chapters 7 through 13, for all the recipes. Happy churning!

CHAPTER 7

The Old Favorite Ice Cream Flavors

Mint Chocolate Chip Ice Cream

No ice cream book would be complete without including recipes for some old favorite flavors. Classics like vanilla, strawberry, chocolate, mint chocolate chip, coffee, mocha almond fudge, and pumpkin ice cream are classics for a reason. Their flavors have withstood the test of time, and they are what we reach for over and over again.

I've also included a few flavors that aren't as common, such as peanut butter chocolate chip, ginger, and toasted almond. But I think they taste so good, they may become your favorites in the future.

Vanilla Ice Cream

This is a basic vanilla flavored with vanilla extract. You can use it as a base for herb, fruit, and other flavors, although the vanilla may need to be reduced or increased, to let the other tastes come through.

> 1 cup (250 ml) tofu
> 3/4 cup (188 ml) oil
> 1-3/4 cups (437 ml) nondairy milk
> 1/8 teaspoon (0.5 ml) salt
> 1 Tablespoon (15 ml) vanilla
> 3/4 cup agave nectar (188 ml) or sugar (150 g)

Combine all ingredients in a blender. Blend for 40 seconds, or until well blended and sugar has dissolved.

Chill at least 2 hours in the refrigerator, or until cold.

Freeze in an ice cream maker according to the manufacturer's directions.

Vanilla Bean Ice Cream

Vanilla beans, although very expensive, make a huge difference in flavor. To save money, try to find them in bulk from a specialty spice shop.

> 1-3/4 cups (437 ml) nondairy milk
> 1 vanilla bean, split and seeds scraped
> 1 cup (250 ml) tofu
> 3/4 cup (188 ml) oil
> 3/4 cup agave nectar (188 ml) or sugar (150 g)
> 1/8 teaspoon (0.5 ml) salt

With the point of a knife, split the vanilla bean in half lengthwise. Using the back of the knife, scrape out the seeds, which are tiny black dots. Place seeds, vanilla bean, and milk in a pot on the stove. Simmer 15 minutes. Turn off heat and let steep 1 hour. Remove vanilla pod halves and discard them.

Combine milk mixture with the remaining ingredients in a blender. Blend for 40 seconds, or until well blended and sugar has dissolved.

Chill at least 2 hours in the refrigerator, or until cold.

Freeze in an ice cream maker according to the manufacturer's directions.

Vanilla Bean Chocolate Swirl Ice Cream

Prepare **Vanilla Bean Ice Cream** as directed in the recipe, above.

Prepare either **Chocolate Swirl or Ripple #1** or **Chocolate Swirl or Ripple #2**, as directed in the recipes at the end of this chapter. Let the chocolate mixture cool as you churn the ice cream.

If you make the chocolate mixture just before you start churning your ice cream, place it in a heat-proof bowl in the freezer, to cool as quickly as possible, while your ice cream is churning.

To make the swirl, remove the ice cream when it is still soft enough to spread, but firm enough that it holds its shape. Spread a shallow layer of ice cream in the bottom of a container. Shallow, wide containers work better than narrow, tall ones.

Remove the chocolate mixture from the freezer, or be sure to use cooled mixture. Drop gobs or drizzles of the chocolate mixture on top the ice cream.

Repeat with alternating layers of ice cream and chocolate sauce. Cover and return to the freezer for several hours, to harden completely.

Or you can create a swirl by dragging a chopstick or butter knife through the ice cream and chocolate mixture. Holding it vertically, move your knife in a figure 8 pattern just a few times.

Don't overdo it, or it will over-mix and you will lose the beautiful swirl pattern. I know it looks kind of horrible at this point, but have faith (and patience.) The swirl or marble will be evident when you scoop the ice cream to serve it.

Place ice cream in the freezer for several hours, to firm up.

Chocolate Ice Cream (Made With Cocoa Powder)

This is a good chocolate ice cream that is not as rich as the one made with melted chocolate. The plus side is that if your tofu and milk are chilled, you can whip this up whenever you feel the urge. The other recipe needs time to melt chocolate and then chill the finished base. But when you want a chocolate fix, you want that fix! This recipe works just fine.

1 cup (250 ml) tofu
3/4 cup (188 ml) oil
1-3/4 cups (437 ml) nondairy milk
3/4 cup agave nectar (188 ml) or sugar (150 g)
1/2 teaspoon (2 ml) salt
2 teaspoons (10 ml) vanilla
1/3 cup (40 g) cocoa powder

Combine all ingredients in a blender. Blend for 40 seconds, or until well blended and sugar has dissolved.

Chill at least 2 hours in the refrigerator, or until cold.

Freeze in an ice cream maker according to the manufacturer's directions.

Rich Chocolate Ice Cream (Made With Chocolate)

If you think chocolate ice cream needs to be rich and really chocolate-y, this is the recipe to use. Use whatever kind of chocolate you prefer: semisweet, dark, or a specific brand. Check the label to be sure there is no milk added.

The downside is that you need to heat the base, then chill it, so it cannot be made when you need to get your chocolate fix fast. But if you make the base the night before, you can have chocolate ice cream for breakfast...it's technically a fruit, right?

1-3/4 cups (437 ml) nondairy milk
1/2 cup chopped bar chocolate (2-3 oz, 65 g) or chocolate chips (90 g)

1 cup (250 ml) tofu
3/4 cup (188 ml) oil
1/2 cup plus 2 Tablespoons agave nectar (156 ml) or sugar (125 g)
1/2 teaspoon (2 ml) salt
2 teaspoons (10 ml) vanilla
1/4 cup (25 g) cocoa powder

Heat milk until it just starts to simmer. Add chocolate and stir constantly until melted. Let cool.

Add chocolate mixture to a blender with the remaining ingredients. Blend about 1 minute, until well blended.

Chill the mixture.

Churn in your ice cream machine according to the manufacturer's directions. If you don't have an ice cream machine, follow the directions in Chapter 5 for freezing.

Chocolate Raspberry Ice Cream

Chocolate and raspberry make a delicious combination of tart and rich decadence. You may decide to strain out the seeds out before chilling and churning the ice cream.

> **1/2 cup chopped bar chocolate (2-3 oz, 65 g) or chocolate chips (90 g)**
> **3/4 cup (188 ml) nondairy milk**
>
> **1/2 cup (125 ml) tofu**
> **1/3 cup (84 ml) oil**
> **1/2 cup plus 2 Tablespoons agave nectar (156 ml) or sugar (125 g)**
> **1-1/2 cups (193 g) raspberries**
> **1/4 teaspoon (1 ml) salt**
> **1 teaspoon (5 ml) vanilla**

Heat milk until it just starts to simmer. Add chocolate and stir constantly until melted. Remove from heat. Let cool.

Add chocolate mixture to a blender with the remaining ingredients. Blend about 1 minute, until well blended.

Chill the mixture.

Churn in your ice cream machine according to the manufacturer's directions. If you don't have an ice cream machine, follow the directions in Chapter 5 for freezing.

Strawberry Ice Cream

There's a reason that strawberry is one of the three classic ice cream flavors. Ice cream and strawberries were born to be together. They're soul mates...or something...

You can use fresh strawberries in season for this, or frozen. If you use frozen, thaw them enough so your blender can blend them without overheating the motor. No need for red dye number 2754 to make this gorgeous pink color.

I find that agave nectar drowns out the flavor of the strawberries, so I prefer sugar in this recipe. But other testers didn't seem to mind the agave version.

> **1-1/2 cups (180 g) sliced strawberries**
> **3/4 cup (188 ml) tofu**
> **1/2 cup (125 ml) oil**
> **1-1/4 cups (313 ml) nondairy milk**
> **1/2 to 3/4 cup sugar (100-150 g) or agave nectar (125-188 ml)**
> **1/8 teaspoon (0.5 ml) salt**
> **1 teaspoon (5 ml) vanilla**
>
> **1/2 cup (60 g) diced strawberries, optional**

Puree the 1-1/2 cups (180 g) sliced strawberries in your blender until they become runny. Add the tofu, oil, soymilk, 1/2 cup (100g) sugar, salt, and vanilla.

Blend about 1 minute, until everything is thoroughly mixed. Taste the mixture. If your berries are very sweet, you can stop here. Otherwise, continue adding sugar, blending, and tasting, up to 3/4 cup (150 g), or until the mixture is as sweet as you'd like. Remember that when it freezes, it tastes less sweet, so your base should be a little sweeter than you'd like the finished ice cream.

Churn in your ice cream machine according to your manufacturer's instructions.

When the mixture reaches a soft-serve consistency, stop the machine. Remove the paddle and fold in the diced 1/2 cup (60 g) strawberries. I like the big chunks of fruit in my ice cream, which turn kind of icy. If you don't, you can leave these out.

Transfer to a covered container and return to the freezer for another 2 hours, to firm up.

If you are not adding the strawberry chunks, churn your ice cream all the way until it's firm enough to eat, and consume carefully, so you don't get brain freeze.

Strawberry Rose Ice Cream

You can find rosewater in Middle Eastern and sometimes Asian grocery stores, or possibly in the gourmet or ethnic food aisle of your supermarket. It is made from rose petals and adds an exotic, extremely fragrant and sensuous touch to this ice cream.

Use the recipe for **Strawberry Ice Cream**, above.

Add **1/4 cup (60 ml) rosewater** to the blender along with the other ingredients.

Continue with the recipe as directed.

Strawberry Banana Coconut Milk Ice Cream

This combination is based on a delicious smoothie I had at a local sandwich shop. It tastes very rich and exotic.

> **1-1/2 large bananas (or 3 apple bananas)**
> **1 cup (120 g) sliced strawberries**
> **1 can (13.5 oz, 400 ml) coconut milk**
> **1/2 cup sugar (100 g) or agave nectar (125 ml)**
> **1/2 cup (125 ml) rice milk or other nondairy milk**

Blend all ingredients in a blender about 1 minute, or until well mixed and sugar has dissolved.

Chill the mixture.

Transfer the chilled mixture to your ice cream machine and churn according to your manufacturer's directions.

If you use frozen fruits, you can churn right after blending the base.

Apple Maple Walnut Ice Cream

This is one of the few recipes that uses maple syrup. But the combination of apples, walnuts, and maple is such a classic, you just have to make an ice cream out of it.

Peeling the apple is optional. I prefer to leave the peel on, for the additional fiber and nutrients (and less work for me.)

3/4 cup (188 ml) tofu
1/2 cup (125 ml) oil
1-1/4 cups (313 ml) nondairy milk
1/2 cup plus 1 Tablespoon (140 ml) maple syrup
1 apple, cored and chopped
1 teaspoon (5 ml) vanilla
1/8 teaspoon (0.5 ml) salt

1/2 cup (60 g) walnuts, chopped and toasted

Combine all ingredients except walnuts in a blender. Blend for 1 minute, or until well blended and sugar has dissolved.

Chill at least 2 hours in the refrigerator, or until cold.

Freeze in an ice cream maker according to the manufacturer's directions.

When the mixture has reached a soft serve consistency, add walnuts. Run the machine about 2 to 5 more minutes, until ice cream has firmed up.

Banana Ice Cream

2 large bananas, or 4 apple bananas
3/4 cup (188 ml) tofu
1/2 cup (125 ml) oil
1-1/4 cup (313 ml) nondairy milk
6 Tablespoons agave nectar (93 ml) or sugar (75 g)
1/4 teaspoon (1 ml) salt

1/2 cup (60 g) chopped walnuts

Combine all ingredients except walnuts in a blender. Blend for 1 minute, or until well blended and sugar has dissolved.

Chill at least 2 hours in the refrigerator, or until cold.

Freeze in an ice cream maker according to the manufacturer's directions.

When the mixture has reached a soft serve consistency, add walnuts. Run the machine about 2 to 5 more minutes, until ice cream has firmed up.

Blueberry Ice Cream

1/2 cup (125 ml) tofu
1/4 cup (63 ml) oil
1 cup (250 ml) milk
1/2 cup plus 2 Tablespoons agave nectar (156 ml) or sugar (125 g), or to taste
2 cups (240 g) fresh or frozen blueberries
1 teaspoon (5 ml) vanilla
1/8 teaspoon (0.5 ml) salt

Combine all ingredients in a blender. Blend for 40 seconds, or until well blended and sugar has dissolved.

Chill at least 2 hours in the refrigerator, or until cold.

Freeze in an ice cream maker according to the manufacturer's directions.

Peach Ice Cream

1/2 cup (125 ml) tofu
1/4 cup (63 ml) oil
1 cup (250 ml) nondairy milk
1-1/2 cups (230 g) peach or nectarine chunks
1/2 cup plus 2 Tablespoons agave nectar (156 ml) or
sugar (125 g)
1/8 teaspoon (0.5 ml) salt

Combine all ingredients in a blender. Blend for 40 seconds, or until well blended and sugar has dissolved.

Chill at least 2 hours in the refrigerator, or until cold.

Freeze in an ice cream maker according to the manufacturer's directions.

Spiced Peach Ice Cream

Use the recipe for **Peach Ice Cream**, above, but add the following to the blender with the other ingredients:

1/4 teaspoon (1 ml) ground ginger
1/4 teaspoon (1 ml) ground cardamom
1 Tablespoon (15 ml) peeled, minced, fresh ginger

Proceed as directed.

Pumpkin Ice Cream

The flavors of fall come together in this comforting, creamy, spicy ice cream. You can use pumpkin which you cook yourself and mash, or purchase canned pumpkin puree, normally used to make pumpkin pies with.

3/4 cup (188 ml) tofu
1/2 cup (125 ml) oil
1-1/4 cups (312 ml) nondairy milk
3/4 cup agave nectar (188 ml) or sugar (150 g)
3/4 cup (188 ml) cooked pumpkin puree
2 teaspoons (10 ml) vanilla
3/8 teaspoon (1.5 ml) salt
1/4 teaspoon (1 ml) ground ginger
1 teaspoon (5 ml) ground cinnamon
1/2 teaspoon (2 ml) ground cloves
1/4 teaspoon (1 ml) ground nutmeg

Combine all ingredients in a blender. Blend for 40 seconds, or until well blended and sugar has dissolved.

Chill at least 2 hours in the refrigerator, or until cold.

Freeze in an ice cream maker according to the manufacturer's directions.

Ginger Ice Cream

1-3/4 cups (437 ml) nondairy milk
1/2 cup (125 ml) peeled, thinly sliced ginger

1 cup (250 ml) tofu
3/4 cup (188 ml) oil
2 teaspoons (10 ml) vanilla
1/8 teaspoon (0.5 ml) salt
3/4 cup agave nectar (188 ml) or sugar (150 g)

1/3 cup (40 g) minced candied ginger

Heat milk and sliced ginger in a saucepan. Simmer 5 minutes. Remove from heat. Let cool. Strain milk mixture. Discard ginger.

Combine milk mixture with all ingredients except candied ginger in a blender. Blend for 40 seconds, or until well blended and sugar has dissolved.

Chill until cold. Freeze in an ice cream maker according to the manufacturer's directions.

When the ice cream has reached a soft serve consistency, about 5 minutes before being done, add the candied ginger. Allow the machine to continue to churn for another 2 to 5 minutes, until ice cream is firm.

Coconut Milk Ice Cream

2 cans (13.5 fluid ounces/400 ml each) coconut milk
3/4 cup agave nectar (188 ml) or sugar (150 g)
1/4 teaspoon (1 ml) salt

Combine all ingredients in a blender. Blend for 40 seconds, or until well blended and sugar has dissolved.

Alternately, you could whisk the ingredients together in a bowl until well mixed and all the sugar has dissolved.

Chill at least 2 hours in the refrigerator, or until cold.

Freeze in an ice cream maker according to the manufacturer's directions.

Toasted Coconut Ice Cream

Follow the directions for **Coconut Milk Ice Cream**, above.

When the ice cream has reached a soft serve consistency, about 5 minutes before being done, add **1/2 cup (50 g) unsweetened, toasted coconut**.

Allow the machine to continue to churn for another 2 to 5 minutes, until ice cream is firm.

Mint Chocolate Chip Ice Cream

If you don't have fresh mint, you can leave it out, but I love the tiny flecks of green it adds. You can also use either semi-sweet chocolate or a darker chocolate. I like the intensity and less sweet flavor of a good quality dark chocolate.

If you'd rather skip melting the chocolate to make the chips, you can add chocolate chips at the end of the churning process. But this is the way commercial manufacturers do it, and the small amount of effort results in a big difference in texture.

> **1 cup (250 ml) tofu**
> **3/4 cup (188 ml) oil**
> **1-3/4 cups (437 ml) nondairy milk**
> **3/4 cup agave nectar (188 ml) or sugar (150 g)**
> **1 teaspoon (5 ml) vanilla**
> **1/8 teaspoon (0.5 ml) salt**
> **1 handful mint (about 1/2 cup)**
> **1-1/2 teaspoons (7 ml) mint extract or peppermint extract**
>
> **1/2 cup chopped bar chocolate (2-3 oz, 65 g) or chocolate chips (90 g)**
> **1 Tablespoon (15 ml) oil**

Combine all ingredients except chocolate and 1 Tablespoon (15 ml) oil in a blender. Blend for 40 seconds, or until well blended and sugar has dissolved.

Chill at least 2 hours in the refrigerator, or until cold.

Freeze in an ice cream maker according to the manufacturer's directions.

To make the chocolate chips:

While the base is churning, heat the chocolate in a microwave-safe container on high for 1 minute. Stir to melt it. If necessary, heat for an additional 10 seconds at a time, stirring after every ten seconds, until the chocolate is melted.

(You could also melt chocolate over a double boiler, but microwaving it is quick and easy.)

Add the Tablespoon of oil and mix well. You will have a runny chocolate mixture.

When the base is almost as frozen as you'd like it, about 5 minutes before completion, slowly pour in the chocolate mixture. When the chocolate hits the cold ice cream, it freezes immediately, and the churning of the ice cream machine will carry the streams of chocolate away, mix them in, and break them into chips and chunks. It's like magic!

Note: You can omit the oil from the melted chocolate. Doing so makes it a little more difficult to pour into the machine, but you get "crunchier" chocolate chips that way.

Adding the oil gives you a crunchy chocolate chip with a bit of chew to it. It's kind of like the outside of a chocolate-dipped vanilla ice cream bar. Try it both ways and see which you prefer.

Coffee Ice Cream

1 cup (250 ml) tofu
3/4 cup (188 ml) oil
1-3/4 cups (437 ml) rice milk or other nondairy milk
3/4 cup agave nectar (188 ml) or sugar (150 g)
1/8 teaspoon (0.5 ml) salt
2 teaspoons (10 ml) vanilla
1 Tablespoon (6 g) instant coffee powder dissolved in 1
Tablespoon (15 ml) hot water

Combine all ingredients in a blender. Blend for 40 seconds, or until well blended and sugar has dissolved.

Chill at least 2 hours in the refrigerator, or until cold.

Freeze in an ice cream maker according to the manufacturer's directions.

Mocha Ice Cream

3/4 cup (188 ml) tofu
1/2 cup (125 ml) oil
1-1/4 cups (313 ml) nondairy milk
3/4 cup agave nectar (188 ml) or sugar (150 g)
1/4 teaspoon (1 ml) salt
1 TBS (6 g) instant coffee granules dissolved in 1 TBS
(15 ml) hot water
1/3 cup (40 g) cocoa powder

Combine all ingredients in a blender. Blend for 40 seconds, or until well blended and sugar has dissolved.

Chill at least 2 hours in the refrigerator, or until cold.

Freeze in an ice cream maker according to the manufacturer's directions.

Mocha Almond Fudge Ice Cream

I had never tasted this flavor before developing the recipes for this book. It happened to be my best friend's favorite flavor, so it obviously needed to be included.

I'm not a coffee drinker nor a fan of strong coffee flavor, so I didn't expect to love it. It's a little more complicated to make than most recipes, since you have several parts that need to be made and combined, and then need to be finished in your freezer.

But the results are soooooo worth it. Now it's one of my favorite flavors, and every time I take a bite, I can see why it's a classic, and worth every ounce of effort that goes into making it.

Use the recipe for either **Mocha Ice Cream** or **Coffee Ice Cream**.

You will also need to make toasted almonds:

1/2 cup (85g) chopped almonds

Toast them in a dry pan on medium heat for about 10 minutes, stirring constantly. Remove from heat immediately. Place in a heat-proof container and set aside to cool, or put them in the freezer to cool down more quickly.

The final ingredient is the chocolate fudge, which you will add at the end, with the almonds. Use either recipe for **Chocolate Swirl or Ripple #1** or **Chocolate Swirl or Ripple #2** (page 74.) Allow it to cool completely.

To make the ice cream:

Prepare your ice cream base and freeze as directed.

When the mixture has reached a soft-serve consistency, add the toasted almonds to the machine and continue to churn until firm, another 3 to 5 minutes.

Alternately, you could run the machine until the ice cream is firm. Stop the machine, remove the mixing paddle, and stir in the almonds by hand.

Working quickly, it is time to do the marbling/rippling with the fudge sauce. Spread a layer of ice cream in the bottom of a container. A shallow, wide container works best.

Add blobs of your cooled Chocolate Swirl or Ripple on top the ice cream. Repeat with the remaining ice cream and sauce.

You can either leave it like this, or do a small amount of marbling now. If you leave it as is, cover it and freeze until firm. The marbling will happen when the mixture gets scooped to serve it.

To do some marbling now, use a chopstick or butter knife and hold it straight up and down. Swirl it a little through the ice cream and sauce in a figure 8 pattern.

This will create streaks of chocolate throughout the ice cream. Do not overdo it, or the layers will just all meld together. You want distinct veins of pure chocolate flavor running through the ice cream.

Cover it and place it in your freezer for several hours, until the mixture is firm enough to serve. Then try not to eat it all at once!

Peanut Butter Ice Cream

Here's another ice cream that is rich but has no tofu in it.

>   3/4 cup (188 ml) smooth peanut butter
>   2 cups (500 ml) almond milk or other nondairy milk
>   1/2 cup (125 ml) oil
>   1/2 cup plus 2 Tablespoons agave nectar (156 ml) or
>   sugar (125 g)
>   1/4 teaspoon (1 ml) salt

Combine all ingredients in a blender. Blend for 1 minute, or until well blended and sugar has dissolved. Stop the blender after about 40 seconds and scrape the sides down before continuing.

Chill at least 2 hours in the refrigerator, or until cold.

Freeze in an ice cream maker according to the manufacturer's directions.

Peanut Butter Chocolate Chip Ice Cream

Make the **Peanut Butter Ice Cream** recipe as directed, above.

While the base is churning, make chocolate chips.

>   1/2 cup chopped bar chocolate (2-3 oz, 65 g) or
>   chocolate chips (90 g)
>   1 Tablespoon (15 ml) oil

To make the chocolate chips:

Heat the chocolate in a microwave-safe container on high for 1 minute. Stir to melt it. If necessary, heat for an additional 10 seconds at a time, stirring after every ten seconds, until the chocolate is melted.

(You could also melt chocolate over a double boiler, but microwaving it is quick and easy.)

Add the Tablespoon of oil and mix well. You will have a runny chocolate mixture.

When the base is almost as frozen as you'd like it, about 5 minutes before completion, slowly pour the melted chocolate in a steady stream into the machine as it turns. When the chocolate hits the cold ice cream, it freezes immediately, and the churning of the ice cream machine will carry the streams of chocolate away, mix them in, and break them into chips and chunks.

Continue churning an additional 3 to 5 minutes, until firm.

Peanut Butter and Jelly Ice Cream

Follow the recipe for **Peanut Butter Ice Cream**, above, as directed. You will also need **3/4 cup (188 ml) jam or jelly**

I like to have chunks of fruit flavor in the ice cream, so I use chunky jam. I also prefer jams, rather than jellies, in this recipe, but both will work.

When the base is almost as firm as you'd like it, turn off the machine and remove the lid and mixing paddle. Add jam or jelly.

Use a spatula to stir in slightly, just enough to marble the jam and leave ribbons of fruit flavor swirled amongst the ice cream.

I like to be able to have bursts of fruit flavor (Peanut Butter Ice Cream with Jelly), rather than an amalgamated peanut-butter-and-jelly ice cream. But if you want a more uniform taste, mix until everything is well blended.

Transfer to an airtight container and place in the freezer to firm up completely, about 2 to 3 hours.

Pistachio Ice Cream

1 cup (4 oz, 114 g) roasted, salted, shelled pistachio nuts
3/4 cup (188 ml) tofu
1/2 cup (125 ml) oil
1-1/4 cups (313 ml) nondairy milk
3/4 cup agave nectar (188 ml) or sugar (150 g)

Combine all ingredients in a blender. Blend for 40 seconds, or until well blended and sugar has dissolved.

Chill at least 2 hours in the refrigerator, or until cold.

Freeze in an ice cream maker according to the manufacturer's directions.

Toasted Almond Ice Cream

It's hard to believe you can get such a rich, creamy ice cream without using any milk, cream, half and half, or eggs. The toasted almond butter packs flavor and richness into every bite of this toasted almond ice cream dream, which reminds me of a candy bar. This one is perfect if you don't want tofu in your ice cream.

3/4 cup (188 ml) toasted almond butter
2 cups (500 ml) almond milk or other nondairy milk
1/2 cup (125 ml) oil
6 Tablespoons agave nectar (94 ml) or sugar (75 g)
1/4 teaspoon (1 ml) salt

1/2 cup (85 g) chopped almonds

Combine all ingredients except almonds in a blender. Blend for 1 minute, or until well blended and sugar has dissolved. Stop the blender after about 40 seconds and scrape the sides down before continuing.

Chill at least 2 hours in the refrigerator, or until cold.

Freeze in an ice cream maker according to the manufacturer's directions.

When the mixture has reached a soft serve consistency, add the nuts. Run the machine about 2 to 5 more minutes, until ice cream has firmed up.

Chocolate Swirl or Ripple #1

This recipe is very simple and only calls for two ingredients. The texture when frozen can be a little more fudgy or icy than the other recipe (Chocolate Swirl or Ripple #2.)

1/2 cup chopped bar chocolate (2-3 oz, 65 g) or chocolate chips (90 g)
1/4 cup (63 ml) nondairy milk

Heat milk and chocolate in a small saucepan over medium-high heat, stirring often, until chocolate has melted.

Remove from heat and let cool completely, or put in the freezer to chill more quickly. The mixture will thicken as it cools.

Do not add this hot to your ice cream, or it will melt it. Let this cool for a while first, or make it ahead of time so it is completely cool or chilled before using.

Chocolate Swirl or Ripple #2

This recipe calls for more ingredients but is also very easy to make. This has a darker chocolate taste, like a chocolate syrup.

3 Tablespoons (18 g) cocoa powder
1/8 teaspoon (0.5 ml) salt
1 Tablespoon (15 ml) oil
1/4 cup agave nectar (63 ml) or sugar (53 g)
3 Tablespoons (45 ml) water

Mix together all ingredients in a small pot, preferably with a heavy bottom, over medium heat.

Bring to a boil and boil 2 to 4 minutes, stirring often, so it does not scorch, or until syrupy and thickened.

Remove from heat and let it cool completely before adding it to the ice cream.

CHAPTER 8

Herbs, Spices, and Unusual Flavors

Herbs and spices are used so often in cooking that the question shouldn't be: Why are they in ice cream, but rather: Why aren't they in ice cream? Mint is an obvious choice to pair with fruits, but expand your herbal palette by trying basil and rosemary, too.

Because herbs are so fragrant, a little goes a long way, especially with something like lavender, which reminds some people of soap or perfume. I don't like lavender in vanilla ice cream (page 91), but I think it's divine when paired with chocolate (page 91.)

You might not enjoy plain Basil Ice Cream (page 79), but give the Tomato Basil (page 96) and Strawberry Basil Balsamic (page 95) Ice Creams a try anyway. You might be pleasantly surprised; those were two tester favorites.

Spices add a little bit of the unexpected to frozen desserts. Chocolate Curry Ice Cream (page 84) is a personal favorite, and the mild heat from cayenne (which can be made as spicy as you like it, or with different chilies) makes Hot-Cha-Chocolate Ice Cream (page 90) a nice change.

So-called vegetables such as tomatoes, cucumbers, corn and beets get to shine, too. After all, some of them are technically considered fruits, even if we don't use them that way in cooking very much. Cucumber Mint Frozen Yogurt (page 87) is very refreshing and delicious, and not something you'll find in your grocer's freezer any time soon, I'm betting. But it's a sure hit any hot summer day.

Almond Coconut Ice Cream

There is a candy bar in the U.S. that uses coconut and almonds and is covered in chocolate. This ice cream takes those flavors and combines them into a decadent, rich treat. It's a little more work than most other recipes, since you need to toast coconut, chop almonds, and make the chocolate for the ripple, but the end result is worth it.

1 recipe either Chocolate Swirl or Ripple #1 or #2
1/2 cup (50 g) unsweetened, grated coconut
1/2 cup (85 g) chopped almonds

Ice cream base:
1/2 cup (125 ml) toasted almond butter
1 can (13.5 oz, 400 ml) coconut milk
1/2 cup (125 ml) almond milk
1/2 c agave nectar (125 ml) or sugar (100 g)
1/4 teaspoon (1 ml) salt

Toast the coconut:

Place unsweetened, shredded coconut in a dry pan over medium heat. Stir constantly until the mixture changes color, usually after about 7 to 10 minutes. Watch carefully once it starts to get fragrant, because it can go from perfect to burnt in a matter of seconds.

Toast it just until it has turned light brown. Do not continue to a rich brown, or the flavor will be too overpowering. Remove from heat immediately and let cool.

Make **Chocolate Swirl or Ripple** (page 74), following the recipe. Set aside to cool.

Combine all ingredients for the ice cream base in a blender. Blend for 1 minute, or until well blended and sugar has dissolved. Stop the blender after about 40 seconds and scrape the sides down before continuing.

Chill in the refrigerator until cold.

Freeze in an ice cream maker according to the manufacturer's directions.

When the mixture has reached a soft serve consistency, stop the machine and remove the mixing paddle. Add the nuts and coconut and mix in with a spatula.

To make the swirl: working quickly, spread a layer of ice cream in the bottom of a container. A shallow, wide container is best.

Add chocolate mixture in blobs in several places. Repeat with more layers of ice cream and chocolate.

Cover and return to the freezer to firm up, which will take several hours. The chocolate swirl will become apparent when you scoop the ice cream to serve it.

Avocado Ice Cream

Avocado Ice Cream

Es Apokat (Avocado Ice) is a blended cold drink you can buy in markets in Indonesia, and Paletas de Aguacate (Avocado Ice Pops) are sold in Mexico, where avocados originated.

This is the only ice cream recipe that does not use tofu or nuts. The fat of the avocado gives it its richness, and it's a great way to use up excess fruit when it's in season. Because every fruit varies in taste and texture (some are more buttery, others more watery), you may want to adjust the amount of fruit to make the flavor more or less pronounced.

I served this at a dinner party, after our grilled pizza (yum!). It was well received by all, despite its unusual green color. Hey, this would be great for a Halloween party. You could call it Slime Ice Cream, or something equally gory.

> **1 cup (215 g) avocado pulp**
> **1/2 cup plus 2 Tablespoons agave nectar (156 ml) or sugar (125 g)**
> **1 Tablespoon (15 ml) lemon or lime juice**
> **2 cups (500 ml) rice milk or other nondairy milk**
> **1/4 teaspoon (1 ml) salt**

Combine all ingredients in a blender. Blend for 40 seconds, or until well blended and sugar has dissolved.

Chill in the refrigerator until cold. If you are using already chilled fruit and milk, you can go ahead and churn.

Freeze in an ice cream maker according to the manufacturer's directions.

Basil Ice Cream

This tastes a little like pesto, because of the basil, but sweet, green and herbaceous. It's definitely different. Try it for dessert after pizza or spaghetti.

1-3/4 cups (437 ml) nondairy milk
1 cup (20 g) loosely packed fresh basil leaves

1 cup (250 ml) tofu
3/4 cup (188 ml) oil
3/4 cup agave nectar (188 ml) or sugar (150 g)
1 teaspoon (5 ml) vanilla
1/8 teaspoon (0.5 ml) salt

In a small pot, bring the milk and basil leaves just to a boil. Remove from heat. Allow to steep one hour.

Combine milk mixture and all remaining ingredients in a blender. Blend for 40 seconds, or until well blended and sugar has dissolved.

Chill at least 2 hours in the refrigerator, or until cold.

Freeze in an ice cream maker according to the manufacturer's directions.

Beet Ice Cream

This one is for beet lovers, or for those who enjoy earthy flavors in their desserts.

1 can (14.5 ounces, 411 grams) sliced beets
3/4 cup (188 ml) tofu
1/2 cup (125 ml) oil
1-1/2 cups (375 ml) milk
3/4 cup agave nectar (188 ml) or sugar (150 g)
2 teaspoons (10 ml) vanilla

Drain the beets, discarding the liquid.

Put all ingredients in a blender. Blend about 1 minute, until the mixture turns bright pink, and there are no large chunks of beets remaining. Chill.

Churn according to your manufacturer's instructions.

Beet-Balsamic Ice Cream

Make **Beet Ice Cream** (above), adding **2 Tablespoons (30 ml) balsamic vinegar** to the blender with the other ingredients.

The vinegar adds a deeper, more complex flavor, but the ice cream won't be quite as beet-y.

You can also try using lemon juice instead of vinegar. It makes a lighter, slightly less earthy flavor.

Bumpy Road Ice Cream

A simple name for an ice cream loaded with goodies. No marshmallows here, so no rocky road, but another classic combination nevertheless.

3/4 (188 ml) cup peanut butter
1-3/4 cups (437 ml) almond milk or other nondairy milk
1/4 cup (63 ml) oil
1/2 c agave nectar (125 ml) or sugar (100 g)
1/4 teaspoon (1 ml) salt
1-1/2 bananas or 3 apple bananas

1/2 banana or 1 apple banana, chopped
1/2 cup (64 g) roasted, salted peanuts, chopped
1 recipe Chocolate Swirl or Ripple #1 or #2 (page 74)

Combine ingredients except the chopped banana, peanuts, and chocolate sauce in a blender. Blend for 1 minute. Stop the blender after 30 seconds and scrape the sides down before continuing.

Chill until cold.

Churn in an ice cream machine according to your manufacturer's instructions.

When the mixture has reached a soft serve consistency, stop the machine and remove the paddle. Stir in the chopped bananas and peanuts.

To make the swirl: Working quickly, spread a layer of ice cream in the bottom of a container. A shallow, wide container is best.

Add chocolate mixture in blobs in several places. Repeat with more layers of ice cream and chocolate.

Cover and return to the freezer to firm up, which will take several hours. The chocolate swirl will become apparent when you scoop the ice cream to serve it.

Carrot Apple Coconut Curry Ice Cream

I know carrots, fruits and coconut milk are in many curries around the world. What I didn't know was how much I'd love this flavor combination. It's exotic but familiar at the same time.

> 1 can (13.5 fluid ounces, 400 ml) coconut milk
> 1 cup (250 ml) carrot juice
> 1 apple, grated
> 1/2 c agave nectar (125 ml) or sugar (100 g)
> 1 teaspoon (5 ml) yellow curry powder
> 1/8 teaspoon (0.5 ml) salt

Combine all ingredients in a blender. Blend for 40 seconds, or until well blended and sugar has dissolved.

Chill at least 2 hours in the refrigerator, or until cold.

Freeze in an ice cream maker according to the manufacturer's directions.

Cherry Almond Coconut Milk Ice Cream

I've had delicious pies made with cherries, almond extract, and blanched almonds. This ice cream takes those same flavors and combines them with creamy coconut milk to create a flavorful, tasty surprise.

1 can (13.5 fluid ounces, 400 ml) coconut milk
3 cups (360 g) pitted cherries
3/4 cup agave nectar (188 ml) or sugar (150 g)
1/4 teaspoon (1 ml) salt
2 teaspoons (10 ml) almond extract
1 teaspoon (5 ml) vanilla

3/4 cup (130 g) blanched, chopped almonds

Combine all ingredients except nuts in a blender. Blend for 40 to 60 seconds, or until well blended and sugar has dissolved.

Chill at least 2 hours in the refrigerator, or until cold.

Freeze in an ice cream maker according to the manufacturer's directions.

When the mixture has reached a soft serve consistency, stop the machine and remove the paddle. Stir in the nuts. Place in a container in the freezer for several hours to firm up.

Chocolate Curry Ice Cream

Yeah, I know, a weird-sounding combination. But it's actually one of my favorites, although I may be partial, since I love both chocolate and curries.

I use a mild, yellow curry powder for this recipe, not a red, fiery one, although I keep saying, "Be the boss of your ice cream." What the heck, try other curry powders if you want!

Use the recipe for any of the chocolate ice creams (**Rich Chocolate Ice Cream** (page 54), **Chocolate Ice Cream** (Made With Cocoa Powder, page 53) or **Chocolate Coconut Ice Cream** (page 131.)

Add **1 teaspoon (5 ml) curry powder**.

Proceed with the recipe as directed.

Optional: You can add **1/2 cup (50 g) unsweetened, grated coconut** as a mix-in at the end, when the ice cream has reached the soft-serve state. Transfer to the freezer for a few hours to harden up.

Chocolate Pretzel Ice Cream

Follow the recipe for any of the chocolate ice creams: **Chocolate Ice Cream (Made With Cocoa Powder)** (page 53) or **Rich Chocolate Ice Cream (Made With Chocolate)** (page 54) or **Chocolate Coconut Ice Cream** (page 131.)

When the mixture has reached a soft serve consistency, add **1/2 cup (40 g) chopped pretzels**. Run the machine about 2 to 5 more minutes, until ice cream has firmed up.

Alternately, you can stir the pretzels in by hand. Transfer to an airtight container and freeze several more hours, until firm enough to serve.

Cinnamon Stick Ice Cream

Cinnamon sticks are dried pieces of bark from a tree. They have a stronger flavor than ground cinnamon and still retain some of the warming heat that cinnamon has. Look for them at Indian markets, in Chinatown, or possibly in bulk in your natural foods store.

5 cinnamon sticks, broken in half, if you can (they can be very hard)
1-3/4 cups (437 ml) nondairy milk

1 cup (250 ml) tofu
3/4 cup (188 ml) oil
3/4 cup agave nectar (188 ml) or sugar (150 g)
1/8 teaspoon (0.5 ml) salt
1 teaspoon (5 ml) vanilla

Bring the cinnamon sticks and milk just to a boil. Remove from heat. Let steep 1 hour.

Strain the mixture. Remove cinnamon sticks and discard them.

Combine milk and remaining ingredients in a blender. Blend for 40 seconds, or until well blended and sugar has dissolved.

Chill at least 2 hours in the refrigerator, or until cold.

Freeze in an ice cream maker according to the manufacturer's directions.

Corn Ice Cream

Corn is used in paletas, ice cream bars on a stick, made from frozen fruit and other flavors, in Mexico. Corn is also used in sweet desserts and snacks throughout Southeast Asia. So why not in ice cream?

2 ears corn
1-1/4 cups (313 ml) nondairy milk

3/4 cup (188 ml) tofu
1/2 cup (125 ml) oil
1/2 cup plus 2 Tablespoons agave nectar (156 ml) or sugar (125 g)
1/4 teaspoon (1 ml) salt
1 teaspoon (5 ml) vanilla
2 Tablespoons (30 ml) lemon juice

Cut the corn kernels off the cob. Heat them with milk until just boiling. Remove from heat. Let steep at least one hour.

Combine the milk mixture with the remaining ingredients in a blender. Blend for 40 seconds, or until well blended and sugar has dissolved.

If you want a smoother texture, strain the mixture and discard the corn solids.

Chill at least 2 hours in the refrigerator, or until cold.

Freeze in an ice cream maker according to the manufacturer's directions.

Cucumber Mint Frozen Yogurt

In many countries, including Mexico, Iran and India, cucumber is used in sweet drinks. The addition of mint and lime makes this different, extremely refreshing frozen yogurt, perfect for hot days.

This was a runaway tester favorite, much to my surprise. A friend keeps saying, "I knew it would be good."

You don't need to peel and de-seed the cucumber. I like the green flavor and color the peel adds, and I see no reason to remove the seeds unless they are very large and tough.

> **1 handful of spearmint leaves (about 1/2 cup)**
> **1 cucumber**
> **2 cups (500 ml) yogurt**
> **1/8 teaspoon (0.5 ml) salt**
> **1/2 cup plus 2 Tablespoons agave nectar (156 ml) or sugar (125 g)**
> **Zest and juice from 1/2 to 1 lime**

Wash the cucumber and cut off a thin slice from either end and discard. Cut the cucumber in half lengthwise and then into 1/2-inch slices. Place in the blender along with the remaining ingredients.

Blend for 40 seconds, or until well blended and sugar has dissolved.

Chill at least 2 hours in the refrigerator, or until cold.

Freeze in an ice cream maker according to the manufacturer's directions.

Date Ice Cream (Fruit Sweetened)

Dates, orange blossom water, and pistachios are a combination found in desserts in the Middle East and Turkey. This ice cream uses orange and dates to provide all the sweetness, without other sugars. The recipe after this uses both sweeteners and dates.

2 c (290 g) dates, chopped
1 cup (250 ml) tofu
3/4 cup (188 ml) oil
1-3/4 cups (437 ml) nondairy milk
1/2 cup (125 ml) orange juice
2 teaspoons (10 ml) vanilla
1/4 teaspoon (1 ml) salt

1-1/2 teaspoons (7 ml) orange blossom water, optional
3 Tablespoons (45 ml) lemon juice, optional

Combine all ingredients, except orange blossom water and lemon juice, in a blender. Blend for 1 minute, or until well blended and sugar has dissolved.

Your blender will make horrible sounds as the mixture is blending. It will be very thick, so stop your blender often and stir the mixture down with a spatula. If you smell your blender motor, stop and wait about five minutes before continuing.

The orange blossom water adds a distinctive, exotic fragrance, but some people find it too perfume-y. Taste some of the ice cream base and see if you like it as is. You can then decide to add it or not, as you desire.

If the mixture tastes too sweet, add lemon juice. If you want to add the orange blossom water and lemon juice, do so now. Blend for 15 seconds.

Chill at least 2 hours in the refrigerator, or until cold.

Freeze in an ice cream maker according to the manufacturer's directions.

Lemon juice cuts through the dense sweetness of the dates. I find the sweetness to be too cloying without the lemon juice. Decide for yourself whether to add it or not.

Chunky Date Ice Cream (With Sweetener)

This ice cream has chunks of chopped date in it, as well as blended dates in the base. Unlike the other date ice cream, this has added sweetener.

The orange blossom water really makes this ice cream shine. It's usually sold in a bottle and looks like water, and it costs about $5 U.S. The fragrance is quite perfume-y, so a little goes a long way. But without it, the flavors are kind of flat, so go out of your way to find some to try in this recipe.

> 1 cup (250 ml) tofu
> 3/4 cup (188 ml) oil
> 1-3/4 cups (437 ml) almond milk or other nondairy milk
> 1/2 cup plus 2 Tablespoons agave nectar (156 ml) or sugar (125 g)
> 2 teaspoons (10 ml) vanilla extract
> 2 Tablespoons(30 ml) lemon juice
> 1/4 teaspoon (1 ml) salt
> 1/2 teaspoon (2 ml) cinnamon
> 1/4 cup (35 g) sliced dates
> 2 teaspoons (10 ml) orange blossom water
>
> 1/2 cup (70 g) chopped dates

Place all ingredients except 1/2 cup (70 g) chopped dates into a blender. Blend for about one minute, until dates are fully blended and sugar has dissolved.

Chill at least 2 hours in the refrigerator, or until cold.

Freeze in an ice cream maker according to the manufacturer's directions.

When the mixture has reached a soft serve consistency, add chopped dates. Run the machine about 2 to 5 more minutes, until ice cream has firmed up.

Hot-Cha-Chocolate Ice Cream

The blend of spices in this chocolate ice cream add a touch of heat and depth of flavor. You can adjust the cayenne to give you the amount of heat desired, or try substituting chopped fresh chilies instead, if you're a real hot head.

Follow the directions for **Chocolate Ice Cream** or **Rich Chocolate Ice Cream**, adding these spices to the blender with the other ingredients:

> **1 teaspoon (5 ml) cinnamon**
> **1/2 (2 ml) teaspoon nutmeg**
> **1/4 to 1/2 teaspoon (1 ml to 2 ml) cayenne**

Proceed with the rest of the recipe as written.

Note: 1/4 teaspoon (1 ml) cayenne will give you a burn at the back of your throat but won't hit you immediately when you put the ice cream in your mouth, like it will if you add 1/2 teaspoon (2 ml.) So use your discretion and adapt this recipe to suit your tastes.

Lavender Ice Cream

Lavender adds a sweet, powdery fragrance to ice cream. But some people find it reminds them of soap. If you don't care for this vanilla version, do try the chocolate version.

1-3/4 cups (437 ml) nondairy milk
2 Tablespoons (4 g) dried lavender flowers

1 cup (250 ml) tofu
3/4 cup (188 ml) oil
3/4 cup agave nectar (188 ml) or sugar (150 g)
1 teaspoon (5 ml) vanilla

In a small pot on the stove on medium-high heat, bring the milk just to a boil. Stir often, so the milk does not scorch. Remove from heat.

Add lavender. Let steep for 1 hour.

Strain the mixture through a fine sieve. Discard lavender.

Add the milk mixture to a blender with the other ingredients. Blend about 40 seconds, until well blended and the sugar has dissolved.

Chill in the refrigerator.

Freeze in an ice cream maker according to the manufacturer's directions.

Chocolate Lavender Ice Cream

Follow the recipe for **Lavender Ice Cream** (above) as directed.

Add **1/3 cup (40 g) cocoa powder** and **1/4 teaspoon (1 ml) salt** to the blender with the other ingredients.

Lemongrass-Ginger-Mint Sorbet

Sorbets are so refreshing because they are basically frozen liquid. In this case, an infusion of lemongrass, ginger and mint, which together make an exotic blend.

If you grow your own lemongrass, the leaves will be plentiful. If you buy lemongrass stalks, they usually have had the leaves cut off. You can make this with the stalks, but the flavor will be much less intense than with leaves.

> **1-1/2 cups (375 ml) boiling water**
> **1 handful fresh mint leaves (about 1/2 cup)**
> **3 or 4 lemongrass leaves or stalks**
> **1 inch (2.5 cm) fresh ginger, thinly sliced (no need to peel it)**
> **1/2 c agave nectar (125 ml) or sugar (100 g)**
> **1-1/2 cups (375 ml) cold water**

If you are using lemongrass leaves, cut them into shorter pieces. I find a pair of garden clippers works well. If you are using the stalks, smash them with the back of your knife, or slice them thinly.

Add the mint, lemongrass and ginger to the boiling water. Remove from heat. Let it steep for 1 hour.

Strain the mixture. Discard the herbs.

Add the sweetener and cold water to the herb infusion. Mix well to dissolve the sugar.

Chill the mixture at least two hours, or until it is well chilled.

Churn in an ice cream machine according to your manufacturer's directions.

This is best eaten soon after churning, because it will freeze rock solid eventually and can be difficult to soften, because it melts very quickly and never really returns to a slushy state. But it's still very refreshing if you eat it the next day or later, after thawing a bit.

Maple No-Bacon Pecan Ice Cream

I was intrigued when I first heard about bacon ice cream. After making this recipe, one of my testers commented, "I took one bite and said, 'No more!'" But I really enjoyed it. It definitely crosses the line between sweet and savory. Be sure to use vegan bacon bits.

1 cup (250 ml) tofu
3/4 cup (188 ml) oil
1-3/4 cups (437 ml) nondairy milk
3/4 cup (188 ml) maple syrup
1/4 teaspoon (1 ml) salt
1 Tablespoon (15 ml) vanilla
1/4 teaspoon (1 ml) liquid smoke, optional

1/2 cup (50 g) chopped pecans
1/4 cup (35 g) fake bacon bits

Combine all ingredients except pecans and bacon bits in a blender. Blend for 40 seconds, or until well blended and sugar has dissolved.

Chill at least 2 hours in the refrigerator, or until cold.

Freeze in an ice cream maker according to the manufacturer's directions.

When the mixture has reached a soft serve consistency, add nuts and bacon bits. Run the machine about 2 to 5 more minutes, until ice cream has firmed up.

Prune Ice Cream

Like the date ice cream, this has a more subtle sweetness that comes from the fruit itself, although this has agave nectar (or sugar) in it as well. Adjust the sweetness to suit your palate.

1/2 cup (125 ml) oil
3/4 cup (188 ml) tofu
1-1/4 cups (313 ml) nondairy milk
1/4 teaspoon (1 ml) salt
1/2 c agave nectar (125 ml) or sugar (100 g)
2 teaspoons (10 ml) vanilla
1 cup (150 g) prunes
1/4 cup water (63 ml)
1/2 teaspoon (2 ml) cinnamon

Combine all ingredients in a blender. Blend for 1 minute, or until well blended and sugar has dissolved.

The mixture will be very thick, so stop your blender often and stir the mixture down with a spatula. If you smell your blender motor, stop and wait about five minutes before continuing. You may add a little water if necessary.

Chill at least 2 hours in the refrigerator, or until cold.

Prune Walnut Ice Cream

Make the recipe for **Prune Ice Cream**, above, as directed.

When the mixture has reached a soft serve consistency, add **1/2 cup (60 g) chopped walnuts**. Run the machine about 2 to 5 more minutes, until the ice cream has firmed up.

Strawberry Basil Balsamic Ice Cream

Another tester favorite. The combination of balsamic vinegar and strawberries is quite luscious. Adding basil takes it to another level altogether, although you could leave it out or try substituting rosemary, tarragon or mint leaves instead.

I prefer sugar rather than agave nectar as a sweetener, because I think the agave drowns out the strawberry flavor. Other people, however, don't seem to have a problem with it. So decide for yourself.

1/2 cup (125 ml) tofu
1/3 cup (84 ml) oil
3/4 cup + 2 Tablespoons (220 ml) nondairy milk
3/4 cup sugar (150 g) or agave nectar (188 ml)
2 cups (240 g) sliced strawberries
1 handful basil leaves (about 1/2 cup), chopped
2 Tablespoons (30 ml) balsamic vinegar

Combine all ingredients in a blender. Blend for 40 seconds, or until well blended and sugar has dissolved.

Chill at least 2 hours in the refrigerator, or until cold.

Freeze in an ice cream maker according to the manufacturer's directions.

Tomato Ice Cream

Another refreshing tester favorite, although I think it tastes like cold tomato soup. If you grow your own tomatoes, this might be nice to try when you have a harvest, but I haven't had the good fortune to be able to try that yet. (If you try it, please let me know how it goes.)

> 1 can (14.5 oz, 411 g) diced or whole tomatoes, organic
> if possible
> 1/2 cup (125 ml) tofu
> 1/3 cup (84 ml) oil
> 1-1/4 cups (313 ml) nondairy milk
> 3/4 cup agave nectar (188 ml) or sugar (150 g)
> 1 Tablespoon (15 ml) peeled and minced fresh ginger
> 1/4 teaspoon (1 ml) cinnamon
> 1/4 teaspoon (1 ml) ground cloves

Make sure the tomatoes you are using do not contain pepper, onions, garlic, or vinegar. Drain the tomatoes and discard the liquid.

Add the tomato pieces and remaining ingredients to a blender. Blend about 1 minute, until well blended and there are no longer large chunks of tomato. Chill.

Churn according to your manufacturer's instructions.

Tomato-Basil Ice Cream

Follow the directions for **Tomato Ice Cream**, above, adding **1/4 cup (half a handful) chopped fresh basil or cinnamon basil** to the mixture in the blender.

The basil adds a heavier, greener flavor. Cinnamon basil has a spicy, sweet fragrance that complements the fruitiness of the tomatoes and spices, but regular sweet or Genovese basil works also.

CHAPTER 9

Sherbets and Sorbets

Blackberry Mint Sorbet

The difference here between sherbets and sorbets is that these sherbet recipes include some nondairy milk. The sorbets do not.

Sorbets usually contain only fruit, water, and enough sweetener (in most recipes) to maintain a soft, scoopable texture. They are very refreshing and popular, especially during hot weather. Strain the seeds--or not--depending on how much work you want to do and whether you mind having a little bit of fiber and crunch, or seeds in your teeth, later.

The sorbets especially can turn rock hard when you move them to your freezer for storage, if they are stored for very long. You may want to thaw them so much that they melt almost completely, then re-churn them. That's the best way to get that soft, scoopable texture. Of course, that takes time. You could always just attack it with a spoon and scrape away.

Blackberry Mint Sorbet

4 cups (500g) blackberries
1 handful mint (about 1/2 cup)
3/4 cup agave nectar (188 ml) or sugar (150 g)
1/2 cup (125 ml) water
1 Tablespoon (15 ml) lemon juice

Combine all ingredients in a blender. Blend for 40 seconds, or until well blended and sugar has dissolved.

If you are using frozen blackberries, you will need to stop your blender often and push the mixture down with a spatula before continuing. Blend until you get a puree and the sugar has dissolved.

If you want to strain out the seeds, press the mixture through a sieve with a spatula. Discard the seeds.

Chill until cold. Freeze in an ice cream maker according to the manufacturer's directions.

Carrot Pineapple Basil Mint Sorbet

Carrots and pineapple are wonderfully complementary. Basil and mint add fresh, green hints and turn this sorbet into a highlight of spring and summer.

1 handful spearmint leaves (about 1/2 cup), chopped
1/2 handful basil leaves (about 1/4 cup), chopped
2 cups (500 ml) carrot juice
1-1/2 cups (375 ml) pineapple juice
6 Tablespoons agave nectar (95 ml) or sugar (75 g)
1/8 teaspoon (0.5 ml) salt

Combine all ingredients in a blender. Blend for 40 seconds, or until well blended and sugar has dissolved.

Chill at least 2 hours in the refrigerator, or until cold.

Freeze in an ice cream maker according to the manufacturer's directions.

Lemon Sherbet

3/4 cup agave nectar (188 ml) or sugar (150 g)
Zest of 1 lemon (about 1 Tablespoon, 15 ml)
Juice of 2 lemons (about 6 Tablespoons, 95 ml)
1/4 teaspoon (1 ml) salt
2 teaspoons (10 ml) vanilla
2-1/2 cups (675 ml) nondairy milk

Combine all ingredients in a blender. Blend for 40 seconds, or until well blended and sugar has dissolved.

Chill at least 2 hours in the refrigerator, or until cold.

Freeze in an ice cream maker according to the manufacturer's directions

Mango Banana Watermelon Sorbet

This is a case where the total is greater than the sum of all the parts. Tropical mango and banana provide creaminess and watermelon makes this sorbet very refreshing.

1-1/2 cups (350 g) mango chunks
1-1/2 large bananas or 3 apple bananas
1-1/2 cups (225 g) seeded watermelon chunks

Combine all ingredients in a blender. Blend for 40 seconds, or until well blended.

You may decide to add some sweetener to this, if your fruits are not very sweet. Remember to make your base slightly sweeter than you want the finished product to be, since it won't taste as sweet once it's frozen.

Chill at least 2 hours in the refrigerator, or until cold.

Freeze in an ice cream maker according to the manufacturer's directions.

Pomegranate Strawberry Banana Sorbet

Feel free to play with the proportions of the fruits to one another.

> **2 cups (240 g) sliced strawberries**
> **2 bananas or 4 apple bananas**
> **1-1/2 cups (375 ml) pomegranate juice**
> **1/4 cup (62 ml) agave nectar or sugar (50 g)**

Place all ingredients in a blender. Blend about 1 minute, or until all the ingredients are fully mixed and the sugar has dissolved.

Chill the mixture, unless you are using chilled juice and fruits. In that case, you can churn immediately.

Freeze in your ice cream machine according to your manufacturer's directions, or follow the instructions in Chapter 5 on how to make ice cream without a machine.

Pear Sorbet

This has a really nice, intensely pear flavor, perfect for fall. There is a bit of grittiness from the pears, which you already know, if you are a fan of pears.

> **2 pears, cored and chopped**
> **1/2 cup (125 ml) water**
> **3/4 cup agave nectar (188 ml) or sugar (150 g)**
> **1/8 teaspoon (0.5 ml) salt**
> **1 Tablespoon (15 ml) lemon juice**

Combine all ingredients in a blender. Blend for 40 seconds, or until well blended and sugar has dissolved.

Chill at least 2 hours in the refrigerator, or until cold.

Freeze in an ice cream maker according to the manufacturer's directions.

Strawberry Banana Sherbet

Strawberries and bananas are another very classic, delicious combination. Adding milk tames the intensity of the fruit down a bit and adds a creamy dimension.

> 2 cups (240 g) sliced strawberries
> 1-1/2 large bananas or 3 apple bananas
> 3/4 cup sugar (150 g) or agave nectar (188 ml)
> 1-1/2 cups (375 ml) rice milk or other nondairy milk

Combine all ingredients in a blender. Blend for 40 seconds, or until well blended and sugar has dissolved.

Chill at least 2 hours in the refrigerator, or until cold.

Freeze in an ice cream maker according to the manufacturer's directions.

Strawberry Rosemary Sorbet

3 cups (360 g) sliced strawberries
1/2 cup (125 ml) orange juice
1/2 cup (125 ml) apple juice
1/2 c sugar (100 g) or agave nectar (125 ml)
3 sprigs fresh rosemary, each 6 inches (15 cm) long

Remove the needle-like leaves from the rosemary and chop them very finely. You should have about 1 Tablespoon (15 ml) chopped herb.

Blend all ingredients in a blender about 40 seconds, or until everything is well mixed and sugar is dissolved.

Chill the mixture.

Transfer the chilled mixture to your ice cream machine and churn according to your manufacturer's directions.

Tangelo or Tangerine Sorbet

I made this after my neighbors gave me tangelos and tangerines from their trees. Tangelos are a cross between oranges and tangerines. You can use anything like that for this sorbet--tangerines, mandarins, oranges, etc. You can really taste the freshness. My neighbors loved it so much, they bought an ice cream machine the next day.

2 cups (500 ml) tangelo or tangerine juice
1 cup (250 ml) water
1/2 to 3/4 cup agave nectar (125-188 ml) or sugar (100-150 g)

Combine all ingredients in a blender. Blend for 40 seconds, or until well blended and sugar has dissolved.

Chill at least 2 hours in the refrigerator, or until cold.

Freeze in an ice cream maker according to the manufacturer's directions.

Watermelon Sorbet

Few fruits are as refreshing as watermelons. When they are in season, you can freeze cubes of watermelon with the seeds removed to have this sorbet year-round.

Adjust the amount of sweetener and lemon or lime juice needed, depending on the sweetness of the fruit you have.

> **1 handful mint (about 1/2 cup)**
> **5 cups (750 g) watermelon cubes, seeds removed**
> **2 Tablespoons (30 ml) lemon or lime juice**
> **1/2 c agave nectar (125 ml) or sugar (100 g), or to taste**
> **1/4 cup (63 ml) water**

Place all ingredients in a blender. Blend for about 40 seconds, until well mixed and sugar has dissolved.

Chill for a few hours, unless you are using already-chilled fruit. In that case, you can go ahead and churn.

Churn in your ice cream machine according to your manufacturer's directions.

CHAPTER 10

How to Make Yogurt at Home

These days, it's easy to buy commercially-made soy, coconut, nut and rice milk yogurt. But they are quite pricey and may be hard to find in your area. Instead, make your own yogurt at home, then use it to make frozen yogurt.

It's easy to do, doesn't require fancy equipment or fussy preparation, and you can make it without adding fillers, preservatives, or extra sweeteners. The bacteria which give yogurt its sour taste also lead to improved digestion and immunity.

You've seen those commercials for yogurt that say they will "help you get regular" and improve your digestion? You can get the same results with your homemade stuff, at a fraction of the cost.

When you make yogurt fresh at home, you have more of the active bacteria alive in the finished product. Because the numbers of these bacteria decrease over time, making and eating yogurt at home means you get the most potent product possible.

What is yogurt?

Yogurt is milk (in our case, non-dairy milk) that has specific strains of bacteria added to it. It is kept at a steady, warm temperature, to allow the bacteria to grow and multiply, which produces a sour flavor and slightly thicker texture.

When we consume the yogurt, the bacteria enter our digestive system, where they help to break down the food we eat. Another important job is to overtake harmful bacteria, such as *Escherichia coli*, more commonly known as *E.coli*, that can cause illness, diarrhea, and even organ failure or death.

Many people believe that foods containing these beneficial bacteria, also called probiotics, help prevent disease and illness. It is impossible to isolate a few types of bacteria in order to find out their effects on health. But studies have shown that people who consume fermented foods, such as sauerkraut and yogurt, may reap health benefits.

For example, a study in Sweden showed that employees given *Lactobacillus reuteri* missed less work due to illness than employees that did not get the bacterium. Several different bacteria, including *Lactobacillus acidophilus*, *L. bifidus*, and *Streptococcus thermophiles*, grow in yogurt and other fermented foods.

Other studies have shown that probiotics help eliminate diarrhea, prevent and treat eczema in children, treat Irritable Bowel Syndrome (IBS), and prevent or reduce the severity of colds. Some people consume fermented foods to help with difficult digestion. Others eat them to prevent and treat urinary tract and vaginal yeast infections. Still others eat them just because they taste good.

Researchers still do not know exactly how our gut bacteria keep us healthy, or how different microorganisms interact with each other. But we do know that having lots of the "good guys" in our gut helps to keep our bodies working efficiently.

How to Make Yogurt at Home

The basic idea is to heat milk in order to kill as many of the spoilage-causing microorganisms as possible. Then a small amount of yogurt, containing active, live bacteria, is added.

The mixture is kept at a steady temperature for about 8 hours, allowing the bacteria to multiply. As they do, they create a sour flavor and slightly thicker texture.

Commercial yogurt made with dairy often uses gelatin (an animal product) to get a thick texture. We won't be using any, obviously, so the yogurt will be quite runny. Since the goal is to make frozen yogurt out of it anyway, a thin texture doesn't matter.

I have used both soy milk and coconut milk successfully using this technique, and a combination of half of each. Coconut milk yogurt gets thicker but doesn't have as pronounced a sour, yogurt-y flavor, for some reason. I haven't been able to make rice or nut milk yogurt, so if you want to use those, you'll need to buy commercially made yogurt, or find another way to make them at home yourself.

Equipment you will need

> **Saucepan**
> **Spoon or heat-proof spatula**
> **1 Tablespoon measure**
> **Covered container**
> **Method of insulation**
> **Thermometer (optional)**

You will need a clean container that is not metal, because metal and acids do not like each other. You can use plastic, ceramic, or glass. The container and equipment you use must be clean, but it doesn't need to be sterilized. Wash and rinse them well and make sure they are dry.

You will also need a way to insulate that container for about 8 hours. You can put your container of milk mixture into something like an insulated foam cooler, a pan with hot water in it, or choose the simplest method, which is just to wrap it with a towel or blanket to keep the heat in.

I wrap a container with towels and put it into a foam cooler. I cover the container, put a towel on top, and cover the cooler. I've also just put yogurt into a covered jar and wrapped it in a towel.

If you are prone to worrying, you may want to invest in a kitchen thermometer. That way you can be sure to use the correct temperatures. But you don't need one. I've made yogurt successfully both with and without a thermometer.

You should be able to find a kitchen thermometer for about $10 U.S. or less. Make sure it has the correct temperature range. You will need to have 105 degrees Farenheit (41 degrees Celsius) and 180 degrees Farenheit (82 degrees Celsius.) Do not get a candy thermometer, which registers temperatures in the 200-degree range, much too high for our purposes.

Ingredients you will need

> 1 quart (1 liter) soymilk or 2 cans (13.5 fl oz/400 ml each) coconut milk
> 1 Tablespoon (15 ml) pre-made yogurt

Directions

Heat the milk in a saucepan on medium-high heat, stirring often, until the temperature reaches 180° F (82° C.) If you do not have a thermometer, heat the milk until just before it starts to boil. You will see steam rising.

Remove the milk from the heat and set it aside to cool to a temperature of 105° F (41° C.) This will take about 20 to 30 minutes in your kitchen. If you don't have a thermometer, place a small amount of milk onto your wrist. It should feel warmer than your body temperature, but not unpleasantly hot.

I tend to leave it and then forget about it, and it gets too cool. If this happens, you can re-heat the milk for just a few minutes, to get back to 105 F/41 C degrees. But watch it closely--this happens very quickly.

When the milk has reached 105 F/41 C degrees, add the 1 Tablespoon (15 ml) of prepared yogurt. This can be from a batch you have made already, or from a commercial batch of yogurt. Be sure the package states, "Made with live cultures," or something similar. The fresher the yogurt, the more active the bacteria, and the better your chance of success.

Stir the yogurt into the milk and immediately pour it into your clean container. Cover it and insulate it.

Set it in a place where it will not be disturbed (the bacteria like to be left alone; perhaps they are artistic, free spirits?...) and where it will be away from changing temperatures. In other words, don't put it next to a window or where it will be exposed to the sun or other heat source.

Leave the mixture there for 8 hours. Check it after eight hours. Using a clean spoon, gently take a small amount out and taste it. It should be sour and slightly thick.

At this point, you can either leave it for a few more hours, up to 12 hours. (I often make some at night, before bed, and let it incubate overnight, while I sleep.) It will continue to get more sour. Or you can consume it or place it in your refrigerator at that point, or make frozen yogurt with it.

Once refrigerated, the bacteria continue to reproduce, but at a slower rate. They will not stop your yogurt from going bad, however, so you need to consume it within about 3 weeks.

Remember to make another batch of yogurt before the batch you have runs out or gets too old. Save one Tablespoon (15 ml) to use as starter. If you forget, you will need to purchase commercial yogurt in order to make more.

How to tell if your batch is no good

If your yogurt has failed, you will see one of two things. Either it will not be sour or thickened at all, or it will be sour and rotten-tasting and may have small bubbles in it and/or look separated.

If your yogurt has not thickened or soured at all, leave it for several more hours and check it again later. If you still have no yogurt, it means your starter yogurt did not have active bacteria, or enough of them, to start this batch. Try another brand, or a fresher product.

If your yogurt tastes or smells rotten, it means that harmful bacteria or other microorganisms (such as yeast from the air) have overtaken the yogurt-making bacteria. You cannot save this batch. Throw it in the compost pile, if you have one, or discard it.

To prevent this from happening, be sure to keep your equipment clean and dry (bacteria love moisture.) Also, you may need to refrigerate your finished yogurt sooner, or be sure your starter yogurt is fresh.

The few times I've had failed batches, it was because my starter yogurt was already on the verge of spoiling. Those microorganisms took over and loved the warm temperature I provided. Instead of making yogurt, I was making spoiled milk.

Stopping the incubation process sooner rather than later can prevent this, if you do have yogurt that is a bit older. Check it after 8 hours and refrigerate it then, rather than leaving it out longer.

You can use your yogurt for other dishes, consume it plain, or blend it into drinks. Or try out some of the frozen yogurt recipes in the next chapter.

CHAPTER 11

Frozen Yogurts

Raspberry Chocolate Chip Frozen Yogurt

Whether you decide to make your own yogurt or use commercially-available yogurt, you will still get delicious results with these recipes. Some people really like their frozen yogurt tart, with a real tang to it. Otherwise, it just tastes like ice cream. So adjust the level of sweetness to your taste.

And yes, you can substitute dairy yogurt for the nondairy yogurt called for in these recipes. They will no longer be vegan, but perhaps you are reading this book just for some different recipes and don't mind if the finished product has dairy in it. You're in charge.

Blackberry Apple Frozen Yogurt

This was a surprisingly harmonious combination of flavors. I tend to like my frozen yogurts a little tart, so adjust the amount of sweetener to your taste.

> **2 cups (500 ml) yogurt**
> **1/2 c agave nectar (125 ml) or sugar (100 g)**
> **1 apple, washed and grated (discard the core)**
> **1 cup (125 g) blackberries**

Combine all ingredients in a blender. Blend for 40 to 60 seconds, or until well blended and sugar has dissolved.

Chill at least 2 hours in the refrigerator, or until cold.

Freeze in an ice cream maker according to the manufacturer's directions.

Blackberry Banana Frozen Yogurt

> **2 cups (500 ml) yogurt**
> **1 cup (125 g) blackberries**
> **1-1/2 large bananas, or 3 apple bananas**
> **6 Tablespoons agave nectar (95 ml) or sugar (75 g)**

Combine all ingredients in a blender. Blend for 40 to 60 seconds, or until well blended and sugar has dissolved.

If you are using frozen fruits, you will need to stop your blender often and push the mixture down with a spatula. Blend until you get a smooth puree and the sugar has dissolved.

If you want to remove the seeds, strain the mixture through a fine-meshed sieve. Discard the seeds.

Chill at least 2 hours in the refrigerator, or until cold. (If you're using frozen fruits, proceed immediately to churning.)

Freeze in an ice cream maker according to the manufacturer's directions.

Blueberry Frozen Yogurt

Like all frozen yogurts, adjust the sweetener to your taste and to the sweetness of the fruit. You can use fresh or frozen berries.

2 cups (500 ml) yogurt
1-1/2 cups (180 g) blueberries
1/2 cup plus 3 Tablespoons agave nectar (172 ml) or
sugar (138 g)
1 teaspoon (5 ml) vanilla
1/8 teaspoon (0.5 ml) salt

Place all ingredients in a blender. Blend for about 40 seconds, until well mixed and sugar has dissolved.

Chill for a few hours, unless you are using already-chilled fruit and yogurt. In that case, you can go ahead and churn.

Churn in your ice cream machine according to your manufacturer's directions.

Pear Sorbet (in Chapter 9, page 100)

Carrot Cake Frozen Yogurt

No, this isn't chunks of carrot cake in frozen yogurt. Instead, the spices, carrots (in the form of juice), dried cranberries, and nuts mimic carrot cake flavors. And the tang from the yogurt reminds you of the cream cheese frosting.

1-1/2 cups (375 ml) yogurt
1-1/2 cups (375 ml) carrot juice
1/2 cup plus 1 Tablespoon agave nectar (140 ml) or sugar (113 g)
1/2 teaspoon (2 ml) cinnamon
1/8 teaspoon (0.5 ml) allspice
1/8 teaspoon (0.5 ml) ground cloves
1/8 teaspoon (0.5 ml) ground nutmeg
1/4 teaspoon (1 ml) salt
1 teaspoon (5 ml) vanilla
2 Tablespoons (30 ml) peeled, minced ginger

1/4 cup (35 g) dried cranberries
1/4 cup (25-40 g) chopped nuts, such as walnuts, pecans or almonds

Combine all ingredients except nuts and cranberries in a blender. Blend for 40 seconds, or until well blended and sugar has dissolved.

Chill at least 2 hours in the refrigerator, or until cold.

Freeze in an ice cream maker according to the manufacturer's directions.

When the mixture has reached a soft serve consistency, add the nuts and cranberries. Run the machine about 2 to 5 more minutes, until ice cream has firmed up.

Chocolate Frozen Yogurt

When a friend, who likes frozen yogurt, tasted this for the first time, she commented, "Hmm. It's tart."

I said, "Yeah, it's supposed to be, since it's made with yogurt, and yogurt's tart." She was used to buying commercial frozen yogurt, which is not the same.

> **1-1/2 cups (375 ml) yogurt**
> **1/3 cup (40 g) cocoa powder**
> **3/4 cup agave nectar (188 ml) or sugar (150 g)**
> **1/4 teaspoon (1 ml) salt**
> **1/4 teaspoon (1 ml) cinnamon**

Combine all ingredients in a blender. Blend for 40 seconds, or until well blended and sugar has dissolved.

Freeze in an ice cream maker according to the manufacturer's directions.

Lemon Frozen Yogurt

This has a light lemony flavor with tang from both lemon juice and the yogurt itself. You can add more lemon juice if you prefer a stronger flavor.

> **2-1/2 cups (675 ml) yogurt**
> **3/4 cup agave nectar (188 ml) or sugar (150 g)**
> **Zest of 1 lemon (about 1 Tablespoon, 15 ml)**
> **Juice of 1 lemon (about 3 Tablespoons, 45 ml)**
> **1/8 teaspoon (0.5 ml) salt**

Combine all ingredients in a blender. Blend for 40 seconds, or until well blended and sugar has dissolved.

Freeze in an ice cream maker according to the manufacturer's directions.

Orange Cream Frozen Yogurt

This is a slightly more tart version of the orange sherbet.

1-1/2 cups (375 ml) orange juice
1-1/2 cups (375 ml) yogurt
1 teaspoon (5 ml) vanilla
1/8 teaspoon (0.5 ml) salt
1/2 cup plus 2 Tablespoons agave nectar (156 ml) or
sugar (125 g)

Combine all ingredients in a blender. Blend for 40 seconds, or until well blended and sugar has dissolved.

Chill until cold.

Freeze in an ice cream maker according to the manufacturer's directions.

Fresh Orange Yogurt

Follow the recipe for **Orange Cream Frozen Yogurt**, above. Use **freshly squeezed orange juice** and add the **zest from one orange** to the mixture before blending and churning.

Peach Frozen Yogurt

You can take advantage of delicious peaches in season during the summer and cut them into chunks. Store them in an air-tight container or plastic bag in the freezer the rest of the year and use them in this frozen yogurt. Thaw them slightly so you can blend them easily in your blender.

You can also substitute nectarines instead of peaches. Adjust the sweetness according to the fruit and how tart you want the finished product.

2 cups (310 g) peach or nectarine chunks (no need to peel them)
1-1/2 cups (375 ml) yogurt
3/4 cup (188 ml) agave nectar or 3/4 cup sugar (150 g), or to taste
1/8 teaspoon (0.5 ml) salt
1 teaspoon (5 ml) vanilla extract

Combine all ingredients in a blender. Blend for 40 seconds, or until well blended and sugar has dissolved. If you left the peel on and do not want them in the finished product, strain the mixture before continuing, discarding the bits of peel.

Chill at least 2 hours in the refrigerator, or until cold.

Freeze in an ice cream maker according to the manufacturer's directions.

Pomegranate Blackberry Mint Frozen Yogurt

Pomegranate juice and blackberries combine to make an antioxidant-rich, pretty purple, tart frozen yogurt.

> 1 handful spearmint leaves (about 1/2 cup)
> 1-1/2 cups (375 ml) yogurt
> 1 cup (250 ml) pomegranate juice
> 1/2 cup (60 g) blackberries
> 1/4 cup plus 3 Tablespoon agave nectar (110 ml) or
> sugar (88 g), or to taste

Combine all ingredients in a blender. Blend for 40 seconds, or until well blended and sugar has dissolved.

Chill at least 2 hours in the refrigerator, or until cold.

Freeze in an ice cream maker according to the manufacturer's directions.

Raspberry Frozen Yogurt

> 1-1/2 cups (180 g) raspberries
> 2 cups (500 ml) yogurt
> 3/4 cup agave nectar (188 ml) or sugar (150 g)

Combine all ingredients in a blender. Blend for 40 seconds, or until well blended and sugar has dissolved.

Chill at least 2 hours in the refrigerator, or until cold.

Freeze in an ice cream maker according to the manufacturer's directions.

Raspberry-Chocolate Chip Frozen Yogurt

Follow the recipe for **Raspberry Frozen Yogurt**, above. While the yogurt is churning, prepare the chocolate.

To make the chocolate chips:

> **1/2 cup chopped bar chocolate (2-3 oz, 65 g) or chocolate chips (90 g)**
> **1 Tablespoon (15 ml) oil, optional**

Heat chocolate in a microwave-safe container on high for 1 minute. Stir to melt it. If necessary, heat for an additional 10 seconds at a time, stirring after every ten seconds, until the chocolate is melted.

(You could also melt chocolate over a double boiler, but microwaving it is quick and easy.)

Add oil and mix well. You will have a runny chocolate mixture.

When the base is almost as frozen as you'd like it, about 5 minutes before completion, slowly pour in the chocolate mixture. When the chocolate hits the cold ice cream, it freezes immediately, and the churning of the ice cream machine will carry the streams of chocolate away, mix them in, and break them into chips and chunks. It's like magic.

Note: You can omit the oil when you melt the chocolate. Doing so makes it a little more difficult to pour into the machine, but you get "crunchier" chocolate chips that way.

Adding the oil gives you a crunchy chocolate chip with a bit of chew to it. It's kind of like the outside of a chocolate-dipped vanilla ice cream bar. Try it both ways and see which you prefer.

Strawberry Frozen Yogurt (Strong Yogurt Flavor)

This recipe tastes like yogurt with some fruit. If you like it the other way around, see the next recipe.

2-1/2 cups (675 ml) yogurt
1 cup (120 g) sliced strawberries
1/8 teaspoon (0.5 ml) salt
1/2 cup (100 g) sugar or agave nectar (125 ml)

Combine all ingredients in a blender. Blend for 40 seconds, or until well blended and sugar has dissolved.

Chill at least 2 hours in the refrigerator, or until cold.

Freeze in an ice cream maker according to the manufacturer's directions.

Strawberry Frozen Yogurt (Strong Fruit Flavor)

This is for those who like to taste fruit with some yogurt.

2-1/2 (300 g) cups sliced strawberries
1-1/2 cups (375 ml) yogurt
1/2 cup sugar (100 g) or agave nectar (125 ml)

Place all ingredients in the blender. Blend about 40 seconds, until the sugar has dissolved and everything is well mixed.

Chill the mixture.

Put the chilled mixture into your ice cream machine and churn according to your manufacturer's directions.

Mixed Berry Frozen Yogurt

You can use any mixture of berries for this, including raspberries, blueberries, blackberries, strawberries, marionberries, or other berry you like. I often use a frozen triple berry mixture from the local warehouse club.

2 cups (500 ml) yogurt
1-1/4 cups (150 g) mixed berries
3/4 cup agave nectar (188 ml) or sugar (150 g)

Combine all ingredients in a blender. Blend for 40 seconds, or until well blended and sugar has dissolved.

Chill until cold. If you are using frozen berries, you can proceed immediately to churning.

Freeze in an ice cream maker according to the manufacturer's directions.

CHAPTER 12

Asian and Tropical Tastes

Baesuk Ice Cream (Spiced Korean Pear)--page 123

One of the joys of traveling, for me, is being able to sample the delicious foods I encounter in other places. It's always interesting to see how different cultures make use of the same foods.

Take corn, for example. In the U.S., we tend to use it to feed livestock, eat it as corn on the cob, or use it in savory dishes. In parts of southeast Asia, corn is used more in desserts and sweet drinks. (You can find a recipe for Corn Ice Cream in Chapter 8.)

I've been surprised by what I thought was lemonade, only to find out it was a drink made of corn, in Malaysia. I've had corn with coconut, in sweet pancakes from a street vendor in Bangkok, Thailand. And I've eaten corn on pizza in Japan.

So what is considered unusual somewhere is perfectly normal somewhere else. The recipes in this section contain ingredients often found in tropical areas of the world, including Hawaii, and in parts of Asia. Fruits such as guava, jackfruit, tamarind, and lychee are featured, as well as ingredients more often considered by some as savory. Those include azuki beans, taro, and black sesame seeds.

I've included recipes for using the fresh fruits, as well as some canned or frozen product. Not everyone has access to fresh, tropical fruits, but you may be able to find something (juice, fruits, or puree) in an ethnic market in your part of the world.

And if you're afraid to try some of these, think about this: If you never try it, how will you know it won't be the best thing you've ever eaten?

Korean Pear

Asian Pear Ice Cream

This recipe, unlike the Baesuk one that follows, includes no spices, so the flavor of the pear comes through. However, because the fruit itself is so mild and watery, the flavor is very subtle in the finished ice cream, and the texture is a bit more watery than other fruit ice creams.

I use the large, brown, round Korean pears. You can substitute one yellow, round Asian pear (also called Apple Pears or Pear Apples), or two of the smaller, pear-shaped, yellow Asian pears.

Also, I recommend using sugar rather than agave nectar, which can drown out the flavor of the fruit.

> **1/2 cup (125 ml) tofu**
> **1/3 cup (84 ml) oil**
> **3/4 cup plus 2 Tablespoons (220 ml) rice milk or other nondairy milk**
> **3/4 cup sugar (150 g) or agave nectar (188 ml)**
> **1 Korean pear, cored and chopped**
> **1/8 teaspoon (0.5 ml) salt**

Combine all ingredients in a blender. Blend for 40 seconds, or until well blended and sugar has dissolved.

Chill at least 2 hours in the refrigerator, or until cold.

Freeze in an ice cream maker according to the manufacturer's directions.

Baesuk Ice Cream (Spiced Korean Pear)

Koreans make a soup-like dessert by cooking Korean pears with ginger and black pepper. This ice cream incorporates those flavors, substituting white pepper, which creates subtle heat at the end.

Korean pears and some Asian pears are round, not pear shaped, and quite large--like a small grapefruit. Use one of those, or two of the smaller, yellow, pear-shaped Asian pears.

Alternately, you can use one or two other pears, such as bartlett or bosc, although the flavor will be a bit stronger than with Asian pears, which have a more watery flavor.

1 Korean pear, cored and chopped
1/2 cup (125 ml) tofu
1/4 cup (63 ml) oil
1 cup (250 ml) nondairy milk
1/2 cup sugar (100 g) or agave nectar (125 ml)
2 Tablespoons (30 ml) peeled, minced ginger
1/4 teaspoon (1 ml) white pepper
1 Tablespoon (15 ml) lemon juice

Combine all ingredients in a blender. Blend for 40 seconds, or until well blended and sugar has dissolved.

Chill at least 2 hours in the refrigerator, or until cold.

Freeze in an ice cream maker according to the manufacturer's directions

Dried Azuki Beans

Azuki Ice Cream

Shaved ice, or "shave ice," as it's called in Hawaii, is a popular snack. Some people like to add a bit of ice cream and/or azuki beans to the bottom of the container before adding the ice and sweet syrup. By the time you get to the bottom, you end up with a milky, sweet, refreshing mixture. This ice cream captures those flavors.

Azuki beans may also be spelled "adzuki" or "aduki." You can buy them dry and cook them yourself, or use cooked, canned beans, often found in a natural foods store. Use the next recipe if you have pre-sweetened bean paste.

3/4 cup (188 ml) tofu
1/2 cup (125 ml) oil
1-1/4 cups (313 ml) rice milk or other nondairy milk
3/4 cup agave nectar (188 ml) or sugar (150 g)
3/4 cup (156 g) cooked azuki beans (half a 15 oz, 425 g can, rinsed and drained)
1/4 teaspoon (1 ml) salt
1 teaspoon (5 ml) vanilla

Combine all ingredients in a blender. Blend for 40 seconds, or until well blended and sugar has dissolved.

Chill at least 2 hours in the refrigerator, or until cold.

Freeze in an ice cream maker according to the manufacturer's directions.

For a nice garnish, reserve some of the cooked (but not frozen) beans and sprinkle them on top the ice cream before serving.

Azuki Ice Cream Made With Sweetened, Pre-cooked Bean Paste

You can buy cooked, pre-sweetened azuki beans in the Asian aisle of supermarkets, or in any store that sells Japanese food. You may find two different textures. 'Tsubushi-an' are not so smashed, and 'koshi-an' are smashed into a smoother paste. They are usually sold in cans, although you may also find the smoother paste sold in plastic bags.

Both are usually very sweet and sweetened with sugar, which you may or may not want to use. If you choose to use either of the pre-cooked bean pastes, use the recipe below, which has reduced sweetener, and adjust to the sweetness of the beans. Remember that the ice cream base needs to be a little sweeter, since it will taste less sweet when it is frozen.

> **3/4 cup (188 ml) tofu**
> **1/2 cup (125 ml) oil**
> **1-1/4 cups (313 ml) rice milk or other nondairy milk**
> **1/2 cup agave nectar (125 ml) or sugar (100 g)**
> **3/4 cup (220 g) azuki bean paste**
> **1/4 teaspoon (1 ml) salt**
> **1 teaspoon (5 ml) vanilla**

Combine all ingredients in a blender. Blend for 40 to 60 seconds, or until well blended and sugar has dissolved.

Chill at least 2 hours in the refrigerator, or until cold.

Freeze in an ice cream maker according to the manufacturer's directions.

Azuki Frozen Yogurt

This is a bit more unusual than Azuki Ice Cream, because the tartness of the yogurt is unexpected next to the azuki beans.

2-1/2 cups (675 ml) yogurt
3/4 cup agave nectar (188 ml) or sugar (150 g)
3/4 cup (156 g) cooked azuki beans (half a 15 oz, 425 g can, rinsed and drained)
1/4 teaspoon (1 ml) salt
1 teaspoon (5 ml) vanilla

Combine all ingredients in a blender. Blend for 40 seconds, or until well blended and sugar has dissolved.

Chill at least 2 hours in the refrigerator, or until cold.

Freeze in an ice cream maker according to the manufacturer's directions.

Azuki Frozen Yogurt With Sweetened Bean Paste

2-1/2 cups (675 ml) yogurt
1/2 cup agave nectar (125 ml) or sugar (100 g)
3/4 cup (220 g) azuki bean paste
1/4 teaspoon (1 ml) salt
1 teaspoon (5 ml) vanilla

Combine all ingredients in a blender. Blend for 40 to 60 seconds, or until well blended and sugar has dissolved.

Chill at least 2 hours in the refrigerator, or until cold.

Freeze in an ice cream maker according to the manufacturer's directions.

Banana Lassi Frozen Yogurt

In India, they make a very refreshing drink from fruits, spices, and yogurt.
This is a banana version, in frozen yogurt form.

> 2 cups (500 ml) yogurt
> 2 large bananas or 4 apple bananas
> 1/2 teaspoon (2 ml) cinnamon
> 1/4 teaspoon (1 ml) ground ginger
> 3/8 teaspoon (1.5 ml) ground cardamom
> 1/8 teaspoon (0.5 ml) salt
> 1/4 cup plus 3 Tablespoon agave nectar (110 ml) or
> sugar (88 g)

Combine all ingredients in a blender. Blend for 40 seconds, or until well blended and sugar has dissolved.

Chill at least 2 hours in the refrigerator, or until cold.

Freeze in an ice cream maker according to the manufacturer's directions.

Black Sesame Ice Cream

My parents used to buy sesame-peanut candy whenever they went into
Chinatown. The candy was diamond-shaped cuts of a mixture of raw peanuts
and white sesame seeds in a stick-to-your-teeth, sugary chew.

My parents would fight over them, but I
hated them, so I was surprised to like
this ice cream so much. It has similar
flavors, especially if you use agave nectar
and add peanuts, in the Black Sesame
Peanut Ice Cream variation of the
recipe.

Black sesame seeds can be found in Asian markets and possibly Latin markets as well. They are toasted before using, and because they are black, they can easily burn. Get more than you need, in case you burn the first batch. They turn the ice cream a most unusual charcoal gray color. Served at a black-and-white dinner party, or at Halloween, this would get a lot of attention.

1/3 cup (50 g) black sesame seeds

3/4 cup (188 ml) tofu
1/2 cup (125 ml) oil
1-1/4 cups (313 ml) nondairy milk
1/2 cup plus 2 Tablespoons agave nectar (156 ml) or sugar (125 g)
1/8 teaspoon (0.5 ml) salt

Toast sesame seeds in a dry frying pan over medium heat, stirring constantly, until the pan just starts to smoke and the aroma has changed, about 5 minutes. Watch them carefully, because they will burn in a matter of seconds.

Immediately add to a blender and blend until they have ground to a pasty powder. Take a pinch and taste to be sure you haven't burned them. They should smell like roasted sesame oil, the dark brown stuff used in Asian cooking.

If they taste burnt, dump them out and do another batch, being careful not to burn them.

Add the remaining ingredients to the blender, along with the sesame seeds. Blend for 40 seconds, or until well blended and sugar has dissolved.

Chill at least 2 hours in the refrigerator, or until cold.

Freeze in an ice cream maker according to the manufacturer's directions.

Black Sesame Peanut Ice Cream

Follow the recipe for **Black Sesame Ice Cream**, above. About 5 minutes before the ice cream is done, add **1/2 cup (75 g) roasted, salted peanuts, chopped**. Continue to process another few minutes, until firm.

Alternately, you can stop the ice cream machine just before it is completely firm. Remove the mixing blade, and stir in the peanuts by hand. Transfer the mixture to a covered container and return it to the freezer to firm up.

Chocolate Coconut Ice Cream

1 cup (250 ml) rice milk
1/2 cup chopped bar chocolate (2-3 oz, 65 g) or
chocolate chips (90 g)

1 can (13.5 oz, 400 ml) coconut milk
1/2 cup plus 3 Tablespoons agave nectar (172 ml) or
sugar (138 g)
3/8 tsp (1.5 ml) salt
1 teaspoon (5 ml) vanilla
2 Tablespoons (12 g) cocoa powder

1/2 cup (50 g) unsweetened, shredded coconut

Heat milk until it just starts to simmer. Add chocolate and stir constantly until melted. Let cool.

Add chocolate mixture to a blender with the remaining ingredients except coconut. Blend about 1 minute, until well blended.

Chill the mixture.

Churn in your ice cream machine according to the manufacturer's directions.

While the ice cream is churning, toast coconut:

Place unsweetened, shredded coconut in a dry pan over medium heat. Stir constantly until the mixture changes color, usually after about 7 to 10 minutes. Watch carefully once it starts to get fragrant, because it can go from perfect to burnt in a matter of seconds.

Toast it just until it has turned light brown. Do not continue to a rich brown, or the flavor will be too overpowering. Remove from heat immediately and place the coconut in the freezer to cool.

When the ice cream has reached a soft serve consistency, add the toasted coconut. Run the machine about 2 to 5 more minutes, until ice cream has firmed up.

Coconut Mint Lime Ice Cream

1 can (13.5 oz, 400 ml) coconut milk
Zest from one lime (about 2 teaspoons, 10 ml)
Juice from one lime (about 3 Tablespoons, 45 ml)
3/4 cup agave nectar (188 ml) or sugar (150 g)
1 handful mint leaves (about 1/2 cup)
1 cup (250 ml) nondairy milk
1/8 teaspoon (0.5 ml) salt

1/2 cup (50 g) shredded, unsweetened coconut

Combine all ingredients except coconut in a blender. Blend for 40 seconds, or until well blended and sugar has dissolved.

Chill at least 2 hours in the refrigerator, or until cold.

Freeze in an ice cream maker according to the manufacturer's directions.

While the ice cream is churning, toast coconut:

Place unsweetened, shredded coconut in a dry pan over medium heat. Stir constantly until the mixture changes color, usually after about 7 to 10 minutes. Watch carefully once it starts to get fragrant, because it can go from perfect to burnt in a matter of seconds.

Toast it just until it has turned light brown. Do not continue to a rich brown, or the flavor will be too overpowering. Remove from heat immediately and place the coconut in the freezer to cool.

When the ice cream has reached a soft serve consistency, add the toasted coconut. Run the machine about 2 to 5 more minutes, until ice cream has firmed up.

Coffee Chai Ice Cream

Chai often refers to a spiced tea drink from India. This ice cream incorporates those spices into a coffee base instead.

1 cup (250 ml) tofu
3/4 cup (188 ml) oil
1-3/4 cups (437 ml) nondairy milk
3/4 cup agave nectar (188 ml) or sugar (150 g)
1/8 teaspoon (0.5 ml) salt
2 teaspoons (10 ml) vanilla
1 Tablespoon (6 g) instant coffee powder dissolved in 1 Tablespoon (15 ml) hot water
1/2 teaspoon (2 ml) cinnamon
1/4 teaspoon (1 ml) ginger
1/4 teaspoon (1 ml) black pepper
1/4 teaspoon (1 ml) cardamom
1/8 teaspoon (0.5 ml) allspice
1/8 teaspoon (0.5 ml) cloves

Combine all ingredients in a blender. Blend for 40 seconds, or until well blended and sugar has dissolved.

Chill at least 2 hours in the refrigerator, or until cold.

Freeze in an ice cream maker according to the manufacturer's directions.

Green Tea Ice Cream

The typical Asian beverage, green tea, is showcased in ice cream form. Because there are so many different types and combinations of green tea and matcha powders and blends, you will need to adjust this to your taste.

Use a high quality green tea in dry leaf form, one that you like the flavor of. The taste of the original tea will be the main flavor, so use something you like.

1-3/4 cups (437 ml) nondairy milk
2 Tablespoons (23 g) green tea leaves
1 cup (250 ml) tofu
3/4 cup (188 ml) oil
1 cup sugar (200 g) or agave nectar (250 ml)

In a small pot on the stove on medium-high heat, bring the milk just to a boil. Stir often, so the milk does not scorch. Remove from heat.

Add tea leaves. Let steep for 15 minutes.

Strain the mixture through a fine sieve. Discard tea leaves.

Add the milk mixture to a blender with the other ingredients. Blend about 40 seconds, until well blended and the sugar has dissolved.

Chill in the refrigerator.

Freeze in an ice cream maker according to the manufacturer's directions.

Guava Ice Cream (Made With Fresh Fruit)

If you have access to fresh guavas, you can make this ultra creamy, exotic ice cream. Unlike commercial guava ice creams, you won't get a bright pink color without using food coloring. Since I don't like artificial color, mine stays pale. But that's okay. The flavor more than makes up for it.

2 cups (500ml) guava pieces (about 6-10 guavas) or 1-1/4 cup (312 ml) pureed, unsweetened guava

3/4 cup (188 ml) tofu
1/2 cup (125 ml) oil
1-1/4 cups (313 ml) nondairy milk
1/2 to 3/4 cup agave nectar (125 to 188 ml) or sugar (100 to 150 g)
1/8 teaspoon (0.5 ml) salt
1 teaspoon (5 ml) vanilla

Remove a small slice from both ends of the guavas and discard. Cut the guavas into smaller pieces and place in a blender. Blend until the fruit is pureed.

Pour the mixture into a strainer set over a bowl. Use a rubber spatula to push the puree through the strainer, leaving the seeds. Discard the seeds.

Rinse the blender to remove any lingering seeds.

Add guava puree and remaining ingredients to the blender.

Blend about 40 seconds, until all ingredients are well mixed and sugar has dissolved.

Chill the mixture.

Add chilled mixture to your ice cream machine and freeze according to your manufacturer's instructions.

Guava Ice Cream (Made With Canned Puree)

We are lucky in Hawaii to have relatively easy access to fresh guavas. Anytime you go hiking, you are likely to come across a tree with fruit for the picking.

But most people aren't so blessed. If you have access to a Latin market in your area, you will probably be able to find canned, sweetened guava puree. The Spanish word for guava is guayaba. You can find flat cans of puree or possibly guava halves or whole fruit in cans.

The puree is already strained, but if you get the fruits, you'll need to puree and then push them through the strainer to remove the rock-hard seeds. Then add the fruit to the ice cream base and adjust the sweetener as necessary.

Using canned fruit will make the base thicker than if you use fresh fruit. So stop several times and scrape the blender down with a rubber spatula so that everything mixes well.

All the canned guava I have seen is sweetened with sugar or a mixture of sugar, fructose, and/or corn syrup. If you don't want to use those sweeteners, you'll be out of luck, unless you can find a source of unsweetened or fresh fruit.

> **1-1/4 cup (313 ml) pureed guava**
> **3/4 cup (188 ml) tofu**
> **1/2 cup (125 ml) oil**
> **1-1/4 cups (313 ml) nondairy milk**
> **1/4 cup (63 ml) agave nectar or sugar (50 g), or to taste**
> **1/8 teaspoon (0.5 ml) salt**
> **1 teaspoon (5 ml) vanilla**

If you are using canned fruit pieces, drain them and place them in a blender. Blend until the fruit is pureed.

Pour the mixture into a strainer set over a bowl. Use a rubber spatula to push the puree through the strainer, leaving the seeds. Discard the seeds.

Rinse the blender to remove any lingering seeds.

Add guava puree and remaining ingredients to the blender. If you are using guava puree, add the mixture to the blender along with the remaining ingredients.

Blend at least 1 minute, until all ingredients are well mixed and sugar has dissolved. Stop the blender several times and scrape the sides down. Adjust the sweetener to taste.

Chill the mixture.

Add chilled mixture to your ice cream machine and freeze according to your manufacturer's instructions.

Guava Sherbet (Made With Fresh Fruit)

8-12 guavas
2 cups (500 ml) nondairy milk
1/2 cup agave nectar (125 ml) or sugar (100 g)
1/8 teaspoon (0.5 ml) salt
1 Tablespoon (15 ml) lemon or lime juice

Cut thin slices off each end of the guavas and discard. Cut guavas into smaller pieces and place them into the blender. Blend until the fruit is pureed, stopping the blender to scrape down the sides if needed.

Place a fine-mesh sieve over a container and pour the puree in batches in the sieve. Use a spatula to press the pulp through the sieve. Discard the seeds.

You will end up with about 1-1/2 cups (375 ml) pureed fruit.

Rinse the blender to remove the seeds, which are like small rocks. Add guava puree and remaining ingredients to the blender. Blend 40 seconds, until well mixed and sugar has dissolved.

Chill at least 2 hours in the refrigerator, or until cold.

Freeze in an ice cream maker according to the manufacturer's directions.

Guava Sherbet (Made With Canned Puree)

1-1/2 cups (375 ml) sweetened guava puree
2 cups (500 ml) nondairy milk
1/2 cup agave nectar (125 ml) or sugar (100 g)
1/8 teaspoon (0.5 ml) salt
1 Tablespoon (15 ml) lemon juice

Combine all ingredients in a blender. Blend for 40 to 60 seconds, or until well blended and sugar has dissolved.

Chill at least 2 hours in the refrigerator, or until cold.

Freeze in an ice cream maker according to the manufacturer's directions.

Jackfruit Ice Cream

Jackfruits are enormous tropical fruits related to breadfruit and figs. The ripe fruits have a taste and aroma remarkably similar to pineapple. The texture, however, is completely different.

The flesh is a bit squeaky and stringy, similar to lychee, longan, or rambutan flesh. Fresh fruit is often sold in pieces, since a whole fruit can weigh 20 pounds (9 kilograms.) It contains lots of sticky sap and can get messy.

Cooked unripe jackfruit is a lot like artichoke hearts, with a meaty texture that can work well in vegetarian versions of pulled pork, for example. It is sold in cans in either brine or syrup. You want the jackfruit sold in syrup for this recipe.

Completely coincidentally, ripe fruit has an aroma similar to durian, the notorious "Queen of Fruits" in Southeast Asia. These are the same fruits that are banned in many public places because of the strong odor, which smells like rotting onions.

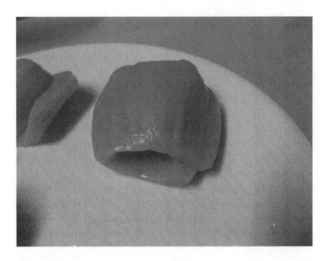

Fortunately, jackfruit's resemblance to durian is very mild, and the taste is completely different. If you can find canned jackfruit in syrup at an Asian or ethnic market near you, give this a try.

1 can (13.5 oz, 400 ml) coconut milk
1 can (20 ounces, 565 g) jackfruit in syrup, drained
1/2 cup agave nectar (125 ml) or sugar (100 g)

Combine all ingredients in a blender. Blend for 40 seconds, or until well blended and sugar has dissolved.

Chill at least 2 hours in the refrigerator, or until cold.

Freeze in an ice cream maker according to the manufacturer's directions.

Kinako Ice Cream

Kinako is a tan-colored powder made from ground, roasted soybeans. It's traditionally eaten with mochi, glutinous rice cakes, in Japan.

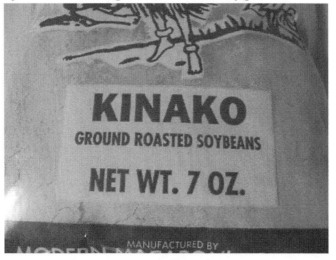

Because the two are found together, eating this ice cream makes me want to eat mochi, too. I can do that, either by making Mochi Ice Cream (see Chapter 13) or by eating mochi with my ice cream, which, to me, is a whole lot easier and just as fulfilling.

> 1 cup (250 ml) tofu
> 1-3/4 cups (437 ml) nondairy milk
> 3/4 cup (188 ml) oil
> 1/2 cup (40 g) kinako
> 3/4 cup agave nectar (188 ml) or sugar (150 g)
> 1/4 teaspoon (1 ml) salt

Combine all ingredients in a blender. Blend for 40 seconds, or until well blended and sugar has dissolved.

Chill at least 2 hours in the refrigerator, or until cold.

Freeze in an ice cream maker according to the manufacturer's directions.

Lilikoi (Passion Fruit) Frozen Yogurt (Made With Fresh Fruit)

You would think that the tartness of frozen yogurt, plus the already very tart passion fruit, would make something that was too sour to enjoy much. Not true. To my surprise, the yogurt kind of mellowed the tartness yet accented it.

At any rate, it is creamy and refreshing, and yes, quite tart. But if you like it even tarter, use just 1/2 cup of sweetener and taste it to see if you want more.

8 to 12 lilikoi fruits, or 3/4 to 1 cup (188 to 250 ml) fresh lilikoi juice (without seeds)
2-1/2 cups (675 ml) yogurt
1/2 cup plus 2 Tablespoons agave nectar (156 ml) or sugar (125 g)
3/4 teaspoon (4 ml) vanilla extract

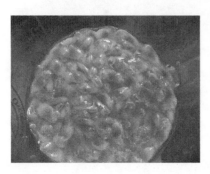

To extract the juice from the lilikoi, cut the fruits in half. Scoop the seeds and pulp out into a microwave-safe container. It will look like frogs eggs in a gelatinous mass.

Microwave on high for 40 seconds to 1 minute, until hot. Blend in a blender for 10 seconds. Empty the mixture into a fine sieve set over a container. Use the back of a spoon or a spatula to push the juice out. Discard the seeds. Rinse the blender.

Put the yogurt, sweetener, vanilla and lilikoi juice into the blender. Blend 40-50 seconds, until the sugar has dissolved. Chill the mixture.

Churn according to your manufacturer's directions.

Lilikoi (Passion Fruit) Frozen Yogurt (Made With Frozen Concentrate)

This recipe uses a commercial lilikoi (passion fruit) frozen drink concentrate, which is sweetened with sugar and corn syrup. If you can't find fresh passion fruit, this will do the trick, although I personally love the fresh, because the aroma as well as the taste are superior. However, I know for most people, fresh lilikoi are nearly impossible to find.

This batch will fill your 1-1/2-quart ice cream maker to full capacity, and it is likely to overflow onto the top rim a bit.

2-1/2 cups (675 ml) yogurt
1 can (12 ounces, 354 ml) lilikoi frozen concentrated drink, thawed but still cold

Stir together the yogurt and thawed lilikoi concentrate.

Freeze in an ice cream maker according to the manufacturer's directions.

Lychee Ice Cream

When I was a kid, just about every house had a mango and/or a lychee tree in their yard. We would spend summers stuffing our faces with fruits fresh from the tree, and we never needed any other snacks.

Nowadays, mango and lychee trees are rare. Most people get tired of the leaves or make space to park more cars. Then people pay to buy mangoes and lychees imported from other countries.

This recipe works with fresh lychee, but you'll need to peel the fruits, which have scratchy skin, and then remove the large, slippery pits. Far easier is to use a can of drained lychee (packed in syrup.) It's also much cheaper than buying fresh, at least where I live.

> **3/4 cup (188 ml) tofu**
> **1/2 cup (125 ml) oil**
> **1-1/4 cups (313 ml) nondairy milk**
> **1 can (20 oz, 565 g) lychees, drained, or about 20 fruits, or 1-1/2 cups (375 ml) meat**
> **1/2 cup plus 2 Tablespoons agave nectar (156 ml) or sugar (125 g)**
> **1/8 teaspoon (0.5 ml) salt**

Place all ingredients in a blender. Blend for about 40 seconds, until well mixed and sugar has dissolved. Chill for a few hours, unless you are using already-chilled fruit, tofu and milk. In that case, you can go ahead and churn.

Churn in your ice cream machine according to your manufacturer's directions.

Lychee No-jito Sherbet

A Mojito is a cocktail with rum, mint, and lime juice. This sherbet takes lychee fruit and combines it with lime juice and mint to make a very refreshing treat. I don't suggest you try adding rum to this, however. Others did, and they preferred the recipe without it.

> **1 can (20 oz, 565 g) lychees, drained, or about 20 fruits, or 1-1/2 cups (375 ml) meat**
> **Zest of 1 lime (about 2 teaspoons, 10 ml)**
> **Juice of 1 lime (about 3 Tablespoons, 45 ml)**
> **1/2 cup plus 2 Tablespoons agave nectar (156 ml) or sugar (125 g)**
> **1 handful mint leaves (about 1/2 cup)**
> **1-1/2 cups (375 ml) rice milk or other nondairy milk**

Combine all ingredients in a blender. Blend for 40 seconds, or until well blended and sugar has dissolved.

Chill at least 2 hours in the refrigerator, or until cold.

Freeze in an ice cream maker according to the manufacturer's directions.

Macadamia Nut Ice Cream

Make one batch of either **Vanilla Ice Cream** (page 50) or **Vanilla Bean Ice Cream** (page 50) as directed by the recipe.

When the mixture has reached a soft serve consistency, add **1/2 cup (70 g) chopped roasted, salted macadamia nuts**. Run the machine about 2 to 5 more minutes, until ice cream has firmed up.

Mango Ice Cream

The best mango ice cream I ever had was in an Indian restaurant in San Francisco somewhere. They used cardamom to bring out the flavor of the mango, making it even more mysterious and sensuous.

Because cardamom is such a strong spice, I've kept the amount on the mild side. If, like me, you'd prefer a stronger cardamom taste, you can add more ground cardamom to this recipe.

You could also take the extra step of steeping whole cardamom pods in milk and straining the mixture, discarding the cardamom. Then blend the remaining milk with the other ingredients and chill the mixture before churning your ice cream. It's more involved, but you get a deeper, more intense cardamom flavor if you do it that way.

At any rate, play around with this recipe. Leave the cardamom out altogether, if you prefer. Be the boss of your ice cream!

> 1/2 cup (125 ml) tofu
> 1/4 cup (63 ml) oil
> 1-1/4 cups (313 ml) nondairy milk
> 1/2 cup plus 2 Tablespoons agave nectar (156 ml) or sugar (125 g)
> 1/4 teaspoon (1 ml) salt
> 1 teaspoon (5 ml) vanilla
> 1/2 teaspoon (2 ml) ground cardamom
> 1 cup (120 g) mango chunks (thaw slightly if using frozen mango)

Combine all ingredients in a blender. Blend for 40 to 60 seconds, or until well blended and sugar has dissolved.

Chill at least 2 hours in the refrigerator, or until cold.

Freeze in an ice cream maker according to the manufacturer's directions.

Mango Frozen Yogurt

Nothing fancy here. Just tart yogurt, orange mangoes, and a classically delicious, almost addictive combination.

> **2 cups (500 ml) yogurt**
> **1-1/4 cups (150 g) peeled mango, cut into chunks or slices**
> **1/2 cup agave nectar (125 ml) or sugar (100 g)**
> **1/4 teaspoon (1 ml) salt**

Combine all ingredients in a blender. Blend for 40 to 60 seconds, or until well blended and sugar has dissolved.

Chill until cold.

Freeze in an ice cream maker according to the manufacturer's directions.

Honeydew Melon Sherbet

This sherbet is reminiscent of the green melon bars sold in Korean markets. The flavor is definitely honey-like, especially if you use agave nectar as the sweetener. Adjust the sweetener and lemon or lime juice to your taste.

Melons are so refreshing in the summer, but you can make this all year long if you cut up the seeded, peeled melon and freeze it in plastic bags.

> **2-1/2 cups (375 g) honeydew melon chunks**
> **1/2 cup agave nectar (125 ml) or sugar (100 g)**
> **1-1/2 cups (375 ml) nondairy milk**
> **1 Tablespoon (15 ml) lemon or lime juice**

Combine all ingredients in a blender. Blend for 40 seconds, or until well blended and sugar has dissolved.

Chill at least 2 hours in the refrigerator, or until cold.

Freeze in an ice cream maker according to the manufacturer's directions.

Mugicha Sherbet

Mugicha is a tea made from roasted barley. It's traditionally drunk in Japan during the summer and rainy seasons, when the humidity feels like your body is

made of adhesive tape, and everything is sticking to you.

Find it sold in Japanese or Asian grocers, typically in plastic bags full of smaller, palm-sized tea bags that you just steep in water. It has a very earthy, almost smoky flavor.

2 cups (500 ml) water
2 tea bags mugicha (roasted barley tea)
1-1/2 cups (375 ml) nondairy milk
1/2 cup plus 2 Tablespoons agave nectar (156 ml) or sugar (125 g)

Put the mugicha tea bags into the water and let them steep several hours or overnight, until it is dark brown and fragrant. To save time, place this your nondairy milk in the refrigerator to chill.

Remove tea bags and discard them.

In a blender, combine mugicha liquid, milk and sweetener. Blend about 40 seconds, until sugar is dissolved.

Chill the mixture if it's not already chilled.

Freeze in your ice cream machine according to your manufacturer's directions, or see the section on how to make ice cream without a machine, in Chapter 5.

Okinawan Sweet Potato Ice Cream

Okinawan sweet potatoes are pretty unassuming looking. They look ordinary on the outside, but inside, they are a vibrant purple and loaded with healthy plant compounds, including more antioxidants than blueberries. Cooking does not destroy the color, so the finished ice cream becomes a pale purple hue.

The ice cream texture is quite starchy and somewhat pasty, although it can come across as velvety. You can substitute other sweet potatoes instead, but you won't end up with the same color. For a nice presentation, fan a few slices of cooked sweet potato across the top of the ice cream.

3/4 cup (188 ml) tofu
1/2 cup (125 ml) oil
1-1/4 cups (313 ml) rice milk or other nondairy milk
3/4 cup agave nectar (188 ml) or sugar (150 g)
1-1/2 cups (375 ml) mashed cooked sweet potato (11 ounces, 300 grams)
1/4 teaspoon (1 ml) salt

Combine all ingredients in a blender. Blend for 1 minute, or until well blended and sugar has dissolved. This will get fairly thick, so you may need to stop the blender after several seconds and scrape the sides down with a spatula before continuing.

Chill at least 2 hours in the refrigerator, or until cold.

Freeze in an ice cream maker according to the manufacturer's directions.

Okinawan Sweet Potato Coconut Milk Ice Cream

For Thanksgiving every year, my father makes a dish with yams and coconut milk. This ice cream uses Okinawan sweet potatoes instead of yams, but you can use other sweet potato or yams instead.

1 can (13.5 oz, 400 ml) coconut milk
1-1/2 cups (375 ml) cooked, mashed Okinawan sweet potato (11 ounces, 300 grams)
3/4 cup agave nectar (188 ml) or sugar (150 g)
1/4 teaspoon (1 ml) salt

Place all ingredients into a blender. Blend for 1 minute, or until well blended and sugar has dissolved. This will get fairly thick, so you may need to stop the blender after several seconds and scrape the sides down with a spatula before continuing.

Chill at least 2 hours in the refrigerator, or until cold.

Freeze in an ice cream maker according to the manufacturer's directions.

Papaya Frozen Yogurt

Some people dislike the strong smell of papaya fruit. But many people can get past it to the sweet, intense flavor. This is the least strongly flavored of the papaya recipes, with just enough papaya to taste, without hitting you on the head with papaya-ness. Papayas are ripe when they turn yellow-orange and give slightly when you squeeze them.

> **1-1/2 cups (375 ml, 350 g) ripe papaya flesh**
> **2 cups (500 ml) yogurt**
> **1/2 cup plus 2 Tablespoons agave nectar (156 ml) or sugar (125 g)**
> **1/8 teaspoon (0.5 ml) salt**

Combine all ingredients in a blender. Blend for 40 seconds, or until well blended and sugar has dissolved.

Chill at least 2 hours in the refrigerator, or until cold.

Freeze in an ice cream maker according to the manufacturer's directions.

Papaya Ice Cream

> **3/4 cup (188 ml) tofu**
> **1/2 cup (125 ml) oil**
> **1-1/4 cups (313 ml) nondairy milk**
> **3/4 cup agave nectar (188 ml) or sugar (150 g)**
> **1 cup (250 ml, 240 g) ripe papaya flesh**
> **1/4 teaspoon (1 ml) salt**
> **1 teaspoon (5 ml) vanilla**
> **1 Tablespoon (15 ml) lemon juice**

Combine all ingredients in a blender. Blend for 40 seconds, or until well blended and sugar has dissolved.

Chill at least 2 hours in the refrigerator, or until cold.

Freeze in an ice cream maker according to the manufacturer's directions.

Papaya Sherbet

2 cups (500 ml, 460 g) ripe papaya flesh
1-1/2 cups (375 ml) rice milk or other nondairy milk
1/2 cup plus 2 Tablespoons agave nectar (156 ml) or
sugar (125 g)
1 Tablespoon (15 ml) lemon or lime juice
1/8 teaspoon (0.5 ml) salt

Combine all ingredients in a blender. Blend for 40 seconds, or until well blended and sugar has dissolved. The mixture will be thick.

Chill at least 2 hours in the refrigerator, or until cold.

Freeze in an ice cream maker according to the manufacturer's directions.

Pina Cobana Ice Cream

Adding banana to the traditional piña colada flavors of coconut milk and pineapple makes an even more flavorful, creamy ice cream. You'll be transported to the islands when you taste it.

Which islands? Whichever you want--you're the boss.

1 can (13.5 oz, 400 ml) coconut milk
1-1/2 large bananas or 3 apple bananas
2 cups (280 g) pineapple chunks
1/2 c agave nectar (125 ml) or sugar (100 g)
1/4 teaspoon (1 ml) salt

Combine all ingredients in a blender. Blend for 40 seconds, or until well blended and sugar has dissolved.

Chill at least 2 hours in the refrigerator, or until cold.

Freeze in an ice cream maker according to the manufacturer's directions.

Pineapple Coconut Milk Ice Cream

The combination of pineapple and coconut milk is pure genius--it's as if they were made for each other. Too bad I didn't think of it. Oh well, I'm glad someone did.

> 1 can (13.5 oz, 400 ml) coconut milk
> 2 cups pineapple chunks (280 g) or juice (500 ml)
> 3/4 cup agave nectar (188 ml) or sugar (150 g)
> 1/8 teaspoon (0.5 ml) salt
> 1/2 cup (125 ml) rice milk or other nondairy milk

Combine all ingredients in a blender. Blend for 40 seconds, or until well blended and sugar has dissolved.

Chill at least 2 hours in the refrigerator, or until cold.

Freeze in an ice cream maker according to the manufacturer's directions.

Pineapple Sherbet

When we were kids, we used to eat pineapple spears sprinkled with salt as snacks. This grownup sherbet variation reminds me of that.

> 2 cups pineapple juice (500 ml) or chunks (280 g)
> 1-1/2 cups (375 ml) nondairy milk
> 2 teaspoons (10 ml) vanilla
> 1 Tablespoon (15 ml) peeled, chopped ginger
> 1/8 teaspoon (0.5 ml) salt
> 1/2 c agave nectar (125 ml) or sugar (100 g)
> 1 Tablespoon (15 ml) lemon or lime juice

Place all ingredients in a blender. Blend for about 40 seconds, until well mixed and sugar has dissolved. Chill for a few hours, unless you are using already-chilled fruit and milk. In that case, you can go ahead and churn.

Churn in your ice cream machine according to your manufacturer's directions.

Pineapple Mint Sherbet

Use the recipe above for **Pineapple Sherbet** and add **1 handful chopped mint leaves (about 1/2 cup)** to the blender with the other ingredients.

You need to chop the mint leaves before you add them to the blender, because if not, they will float in the liquid and just go around and around and not get chopped up.

Tamarind Sorbet

Tamarind is a fruit that is used to give a sour flavor to dishes in Indian and Southeast Asian cuisine. It's also used to make refreshing, sweet-sour drinks.

Do not buy tamarind labeled "Sweet Tamarind," in a nice box, in whole pods. You want the kind that is sold in a block of black, dried fruit pulp.

1/4 cup (75 g) tamarind pulp
1 cup (250 ml) hot water

3/4 cup agave nectar (188 ml) or sugar (150 g)
2 cups (500 ml) water
1/8 teaspoon (0.5 ml) salt

Combine the tamarind pulp and hot water. Let sit 30 minutes. Use a spatula to press the pulp and liquid through a strainer, leaving the seeds behind. Discard the seeds.

Combine all ingredients in a blender. Blend for 40 seconds, or until well blended and sugar has dissolved.

Chill at least 2 hours in the refrigerator, or until cold.

Freeze in an ice cream maker according to the manufacturer's directions.

Taro Ice Cream

Taro is the starchy, potato-like vegetable used to make Hawaiian poi. You can buy frozen, cooked balls in Asian markets, labeled boiled taro, araimo or imo.

The starch gives this ice cream a very smooth, velvety texture. A friend ate Taro Ice Cream in China and loved it. This was a tester favorite, but I almost threw the batch out when I tasted it. Different treats for different peeps.

Half a 16-ounce (454-gram) package frozen taro balls (about 13 balls) or 1 cup (250 ml) of cooked taro

1/2 cup (125 ml) oil
3/4 cup (188 ml) tofu
1-1/4 cups (313 ml) nondairy milk
1/2 cup plus 2 Tablespoons agave nectar (156 ml) or sugar (125 g)
1 teaspoon (5 ml) vanilla
1/4 teaspoon (1 ml) salt
1/2 teaspoon (2 ml) cinnamon

Microwave the taro balls for 2 minutes on high. Drain the water that forms. Combine taro and remaining ingredients in a blender. Blend for 1 minute, or until well blended and sugar has dissolved.

Chill at least 2 hours in the refrigerator, or until cold.

Freeze in an ice cream maker according to the manufacturer's directions.

Tropical Sherbet

2 cups (500 ml) pineapple-mango juice
1 large banana or 2 apple bananas
1 Tablespoon (15 ml) peeled and minced fresh ginger
3/4 cup agave nectar (188 ml) or sugar (150 g)
1-1/2 cups (375 ml) nondairy milk
1/8 teaspoon (0.5 ml) salt

Combine all ingredients in a blender. Blend for 40 seconds, or until well blended and sugar has dissolved.

Chill at least 2 hours in the refrigerator, or until cold.

Freeze in an ice cream maker according to the manufacturer's directions.

Pumpkin Ice Cream (in Chapter 7, page 62)

CHAPTER 13

Mochi Ice Cream

Yes, Mochi Ice Cream deserves a chapter all by itself, because there is a lot of work involved in making it. It's not difficult, but it is time consuming and can be frustratingly finicky and messy, so I'll explain it in great detail.

If you have never had mochi ice cream before, you might wonder what all the fuss is about. If you've had it and can't find a vegan version, you may be jumping with excitement at the prospect of finally being able to eat some again.

Mochi ice cream is not ice cream with mochi in it. It's the opposite: mochi "skins" wrapped around ice cream.

What is mochi?

Mochi is the Japanese name for a rice "cake" made from glutinous, or sticky, rice. Traditionally, mochi is made every year to celebrate the New Year and is eaten just after sunrise on January 1. Families make mochi as part of their holiday activities.

To make mochi, glutinous rice is steamed and pounded in large tubs using gigantic wooden mallets. Typically, two men take turns alternately swinging the hammers to hit the mochi in the tub, being careful not to whack each other.

To make it even more dangerous, often a woman will be squatting below, with a bucket of water. She dips her hand in the water, then brings it up to the mochi being pounded and quickly flips it over in between hammer blows, being careful not to get whalloped.

Obviously, timing and trust are huge factors in the success of the product.

Once the mochi rice has been sufficiently pounded, it turns to a gluey, sticky blob. Women take this to a work area dusted with starch (usually potato starch, *katakuriko*, in Japanese.)

They pull small portions of the steaming mochi with their bare hands and form it into balls. They are dusted with starch to prevent sticking and eaten later for good luck in the new year.

Mochi is also eaten in other parts of Southeast Asia, although it goes by other names. Often it is formed into layered cakes with various colors or flavors, or served with a sweet syrup or other sweetened fruits and vegetables.

Glutinous rice is used a lot as a dessert without being pounded into cakes. You may have had Sticky Rice with Mango in Thailand, or *Bubur Pulot Hitam*, Black Sticky Rice Pudding, in Malaysia or Singapore. (Find a recipe on my blog.) Both are served with sweetened coconut milk.

The texture of mochi and mochi rice

There is not much flavor to mochi or glutinous rice. The excitement mostly comes from the texture. As the name may imply, glutinous rice produces a gluey, sticky, chewy, rubbery end product. Sticky rice is like chewy grains, but cakes of sticky rice become masses of chew.

If you've never eaten mochi in some form before, I suggest using a small batch of this recipe to begin with. For some people who have not grown up eating it, the texture can be off-putting and strange, especially in its sweet form.

But for those of us who love mochi, the chewiness is what's so much fun. When it's paired with ice cream, that texture is contrasted drastically with the creaminess inside.

How to make mochi

We're lucky, because we do not need to get the hammer out and pound steamed rice to make mochi…although that is always an option. We'll resort to the miracle of modern technology and start with glutinous rice flour, also known as mochi flour or *mochiko*, the Japanese name for it. It is also called sweet rice flour, sweet glutinous rice flour, or glutinous rice powder.

You can find it sold in boxes or bags in Asian groceries, and possibly also in the Asian food aisle of your local grocery store. You will be able to find it anywhere there is a population of Asian people, such as Chinatown, because it is a commonly used product.

The texture can be somewhat grainy, especially once you've mixed it with liquid, but once it has been cooked, the starch and liquid turn into gluey goop. Basically, we add liquid and sweetener to the mochi flour, mix and heat it, and we end up with mochi, ready to be formed.

how to make mochi ice cream

Here are the basics, which we'll cover in step-by-step detail later:

Step 1: Make your ice cream

I recommend using a full-fat ice cream for this, not a sherbet, sorbet or frozen yogurt. The ice cream does not melt as quickly as the other products, which is very important to the success of your mochi ice cream.

Step 2: Freeze your ice cream to a scoopable stage. Scoop out balls and freeze them until solid.

Step 3: Make your mochi dough and let it cool enough to handle.

Step 4: Form your mochi skins and let them cool completely.

Step 5: Remove your ice cream from the freezer and work quickly to wrap the mochi around the ice cream.

Step 6: Return to the freezer to allow the ice cream to freeze until firm.

Step 7: Consume it at that time, or, if consuming at a later date, take the mochi ice cream out of the freezer a few minutes before serving, to allow it to soften enough to eat.

Now let's look at the entire process step-by-step, and you can make some for yourself. Allow about 2 hours for the entire forming process. That doesn't include making the ice cream ahead of time, freezing it solid, or freezing the mochi ice cream after it has been made.

Step 1: Make the ice cream

Prepare one batch of the ice cream recipe of your choice. This can be any of the full-fat versions, soy-, coconut milk-, or nut-based ice creams.

Some suggested flavors:

Kinako Ice Cream (Kinako is typically eaten as a powder sprinkled on mochi.)

Azuki Bean Ice Cream (Azuki bean paste is often used as a filling inside mochi.)

Strawberry Ice Cream (A common modern version of mochi has a whole strawberry inside.)

Peanut Butter Ice Cream (Another modern version of mochi has a peanut butter filling.)

Green Tea Ice Cream (Another Asian flavor, and green tea is often drunk when consuming mochi.)

Black Sesame Ice Cream (*Jin Doi* is a deep fried Chinese mochi ball with a sweetened sesame seed and coconut filling.)

Coconut Ice Cream with Toasted Coconut

Step 2: Freeze your ice cream

Once your ice cream is frozen enough to easily scoop it without it melting all over the place, scoop out balls the size of a ping pong/table tennis ball or a walnut in the shell.

Squeeze the scoops of ice cream in your clean hand, or press them down firmly as you scoop them, to make them more ball-shaped and compact. This will prevent them from melting quickly, which will be important when you shape the mochi around them later.

Place the ice cream balls in a container or on a plate and return to the freezer to harden completely. I recommend doing this the night before you plan to make mochi ice cream.

Step 3: Make your mochi dough and let it cool enough to handle

This recipe makes enough mochi dough for 6 skins, enough to cover 6 small balls of ice cream. I prefer making this small batch, because it is much more manageable with so little. It's easier to stir, and you will need to work extremely quickly, so it's more efficient to work with a small batch at a time.

There are two amounts listed if you are measuring your mochi flour with a measuring cup. The difference is that the *mochiko*, or sweet rice flour, that I used, was grittier than the glutinous rice flour. The *mochiko* was a Japanese product; the glutinous rice flour was from Thailand.

To see how much you'll need, take a pinch of the flour and rub it between your fingers and thumb. If there is any grainy-ness or grittiness, use the smaller amount. If it's very silky and fine, use the larger amount.

If you are using a scale, the weight measurement is the same whichever type you use.

Mochi Sweetened With Sugar

     3/4 cup (130 g) mochiko, mochi flour, or 1-1/4 cup (130 g) glutinous rice flour
     1/3 cup (80 g) sugar
     2/3 cup (167 ml) water

Mochi Sweetened With Agave Nectar

     3/4 cup (130 g) mochiko, mochi flour, or 1-1/4 cup (130 g) glutinous rice flour
     1/3 cup (85 ml) agave nectar
     1/2 cup (125 ml) water

You will also need some starch, about one handful (1/2 cup), such as cornstarch, tapioca starch, rice starch, or potato starch, to keep the mochi from sticking to everything.

In a microwave-safe bowl, mix together mochi flour, sweetener, and water. Use a fork to break up all the lumps.

Microwave on high for 2 minutes. If you don't have a microwave, sorry, you're out of luck, unless you have a way to make fresh mochi, such as a mochi machine.

Stir well with the fork.

Microwave on high an additional 1 minute.

Stir well. The mixture should be rubbery and extremely sticky. If it is more like paste, microwave another 30 seconds, and check it again.

The color will also change, from an opaque white, to a slightly transparent, off white color. As it sits, you may see the surface start to look like a plastic skin, somewhat shiny and dry.

Let the mochi dough cool enough so you can handle it, approximately 15 to 30 minutes or so.

Step 4: Form your mochi skins and let them cool completely

Sprinkle a generous layer of starch on your countertop, and spread it around with the palm of your hand so it completely covers the area you will be working on.

When the mochi mixture is cool enough to handle, scrape and pull it out of the bowl onto the starch-covered work area.

You can either break off pieces with your hand, or use a plastic knife to cut the dough. For some reason, mochi won't stick as much to plastic knives, as opposed to metal knives.

Divide the dough into 6 pieces.

With clean, dry hands, dust your hands with a light coating of starch. You want to use enough starch so the mochi doesn't stick to you or the countertop, but not so much that it won't stick to itself, so be careful as you work. You'll get the hang of it as you do it more and more.

Fold the mochi back on itself to get as close to a round or square shape as possible. Try to touch un-starched mochi to un-starched mochi areas, so they will stick well together.

With your fingers, pinch the dough and pull it gently to make as close to a flat circle as you can. You want to pinch the edges so they are a little bit thinner than the center, if possible.

Try to get a circle that is about 3 inches (7.5 cm) across. The dough will shrink a bit when you put it down on the counter, but aim for that size.

Be gentle so that you don't poke a hole in the center. Try to leave that area a little thicker than the edges, because your ice cream will go there. If there is a hole, the ice cream will melt and leak out through it, ruining your lovely mochi ice cream.

Once you have the mochi circles all made, leave them to cool. If you try to fill them while they are still warm, they will melt the ice cream and you won't be able to seal them closed. But if you wait until the dough is too cool, it won't be as elastic, so shape them (but don't fill them) while they are still a bit warm.

Step 5: Wrap the mochi around the ice cream

When the mochi skins have cooled, get your ice cream balls from the freezer. They need to be frozen as hard and cold as possible for this to work. If they are soft, don't even attempt to do this. You will fail miserably and make a frustrating mess.

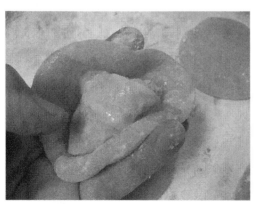

To make the mochi ice cream, lightly dust your clean, dry hands with starch. Pick up one dough circle skin and place it in the palm of one hand. Use a spoon to scoop up one ball of frozen ice cream. Try not to touch it with your hand, because your body heat will make the ice cream melt. Working as quickly as you can, place the ice cream ball in the center of the dough.

Carefully pull the outer edges of the dough over the ice cream ball so they meet in the center, wrapping around it. Pinch and pinch and pinch the dough some more, to completely and firmly close it around the ice cream. Mochi will stick to itself, so you want to try to pull mochi that has no starch on it to another area of mochi with no starch on it, so they will stick together firmly. But you are also trying to do it so the mochi doesn't stick to your fingers, either.

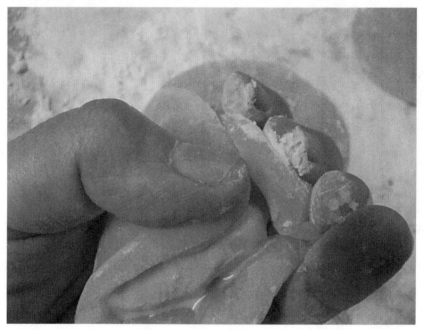

Here is where you will have the most difficulty. If your ice cream starts to liquefy, the moisture will make the mochi not stick together, and you will end up with a handful of soft dough and a melted puddle of ice cream sliding around on it.

In that case, eat it or put it into the freezer so the ice cream can firm up. You'll still have a mess in your freezer, and you will never be able to shape that into a proper ball, but it will still taste good.

If all goes well, you will work frantically to pinch the mochi shut around the ice cream, and it will stay shut. That's why you don't want too much starch. Too much, and the mochi won't stick.

Step 6: Freeze until firm

As soon as you have the mochi sealed, place it in the freezer, preferably on a plate or other clean, dry, flat surface. I prefer to keep the seam up, because if it starts to unwrap, it makes less of a mess than if the seam were down, allowing all the ice cream to leak out the bottom.

You will have some failures, especially in the beginning, as you learn to do this. But try to figure out what is causing the problem, and persist. Because it's not difficult to do. In fact, it's kind of fun. It's sort of like playing with play dough as a child.

It's challenging, for sure. Tricky, messy, yes. But do-able.

Once you have made one mochi ice cream, jump into making the next one. You might prefer to keep the ice cream balls in the freezer and retrieve them one at a time, to keep them as cold and hard as possible.

After you have made the completed, ice-cream-filled mochi balls, place them in the freezer for the ice cream to firm up again. This takes about two hours.

Step 7: Consume now or later

At this point, you can eat the mochi ice cream. If you decide to keep them for later, let them freeze an additional hour or more, until they are hard as rocks, and transfer them to an airtight container or plastic bag.

When you are ready to eat the mochi ice cream, take them out of the freezer and allow them to soften for about 15 minutes. The mochi will have turned very hard, and you won't be able to eat it right away.

These will keep fine for several days. However, for some reason, the mochi sweetened with agave nectar will not last as long in the freezer before getting unpleasantly stiff.

It's like when you refrigerate cooked rice. You can take the rice out of the refrigerator the next day, and it will be cold but not stiff. Wait another day, and the rice will have gotten stiff. Some kind of chemical change happens when the starch in the rice meets the colder temperatures.

The same thing is happening with the mochi. For a couple days, when you thaw it to eat, the mochi skins will soften back to chewy, pliable goodness. But wait too many days to eat it, and the mochi sweetened with agave becomes stiff, even when thawed.

I don't know why, and I don't know a way to prevent this. So if you use agave nectar, plan to eat your completed mochi ice creams within a few days.

The only alternative I can think of is to remove the ice cream and serve it separately. Place the too-hard mochi skins in a bowl in the microwave with a sprinkling of water. Heat on high until you see them puff and rise up. Stop the microwave and let them cool (they will be extremely hot.) Serve the mochi and ice cream in separate dishes, so the mochi won't melt the ice cream.

Mochi Ice Cream Troubleshooting

Here are the most common problems you are likely to run into while making mochi ice cream:

Problem: The mochi is sticking to everything.

Try this: Make sure you have enough starch covering your work surface and hands. If you get some mochi on your hands, take the time to wash it off, dry your hands, and put starch on your hands before trying to make the next piece.

The mochi sticks to itself best of all. Once you have some on your hands, you too will start to stick to everything. You will tear holes in the dough as you work, and the dough will stick to your fingers instead of staying closed when you pinch it.

Also, make sure you have cooked it long enough in the microwave. If it's undercooked, it won't come together.

If all else fails, next time, add a little more mochi flour when you mix your mochi dough. Write down how much you are using. Every brand is different, so you might need to adjust that. But the recipe as written should get you pretty close; it's not so finicky that you need to have perfect proportions and measurements.

Problem: The ice cream is melting too fast and I can't close the mochi.

Try this: Place the ice cream balls back into the freezer until they are hard. Then take only one ball out of the freezer at a time. Work quickly and neatly, and with practice, you should get it.

If you just can't seem to make it work, try a different ice cream recipe. Some tend to melt more quickly than others, and you may have better luck with a different flavor.

Problem: I keep getting holes in the dough, and the ice cream leaks out.

Try this: Be careful and gentle as you work with the dough. If necessary, use smaller balls of ice cream so there is lots of dough to go around and cover the ice cream easily without you struggling with it. Better to have less ice cream with a lot of mochi around it, than nothing but a mess to show for all your efforts.

Problem: I made the mochi ice cream all right, but in the freezer, they opened up and leaked.

Try this: Make sure to pinch the opening many times tightly until it is completely closed, and use as little starch as possible on the edges, so the dough will stick to itself. Place the completed balls in the coldest part of the freezer, so they harden up quickly.

Problem: This is too much work, and it's not working. I give up!

Try this: Okay, I hear you. Now you know why it costs so much. Try eating your ice cream and throwing a slab of mochi, or smaller bits of mochi, on top. You get a similar chewy and creamy combination, with a lot less work.

How to Clean Up Afterwards

Mochi sticks to everything, and you may be freaking out about how you will get your utensils and bowls clean when you're done. But don't worry.

Soak the bowls and utensils in water for several hours. The starch will soften and the mochi will almost all melt off.

To clean mochi off the countertop, sprinkle a little water on sticky globs and leave them there a few minutes, to loosen. Then come back with a stiff rubber or plastic spatula (one that won't scratch your countertop) and scrape the gob off. The rest will come off with a damp cloth.

You can also use a sprinkling of baking powder like you would scouring powder. Use a barely damp cloth or sponge with dry baking powder to scrub the mochi off easily, without scratching. It works like magic.

Ideas and Inspiration

New Year's Eve

Try making mochi ice cream at your next New Year's Eve party. You can freeze the ice cream balls ahead of time, so they are ready to go. At about 8 pm, make the mochi dough. After it cools enough to handle, invite your guests to come shape their own mochi for mochi ice cream.

Only the adventurous and fun-loving will want to attempt it, but many people enjoy shaping the mochi and getting their hands dirty. Place the finished mochi into the freezer to harden. Just after the stroke of midnight, bring them out to enjoy, and get your shot of good luck for the new year.

You can always forego the wrapping around the ice cream part. Instead, have your guests make tiny mochi balls or smaller bits from the dough. To eat, scoop out ice cream into bowls, and top each serving with one mochi ball or a few mochi bits. You still get the chewy and creamy combination, but without the mess and fuss.

Ice Cream Buffet with Mochi Topping

Try serving a selection of Asian-flavored ice creams with small pieces of mochi as a topping. Kind of like an Asian sundae party.

Azuki Bean, Black Sesame Seed, Green Tea, Kinako, Baesuk (Korean Pear), Ginger, Lychee, Okinawan Sweet Potato, Taro, or Coffee Ice Creams, or any of the coconut-based ice creams would all work well and be exotic and interesting enough for even the most adventurous guest.

If you want to offer other toppings, try chopped nuts, toasted, grated coconut, black sesame seeds, cooked azuki beans, small pineapple chunks, pieces of candied ginger, and kinako powder. And then invite me…I'd love to come!

Using a Mochi Machine

If you have a mochi making machine, you can use it to make your mochi dough, rather than starting with glutinous rice flour. Using mochi rice, cook and mix it with the mochi machine to make mochi dough. Follow your manufacturer's directions.

Once the dough is done, allow it to cool enough to handle, and proceed as above to form skins and wrap the ice cream balls.

Brown Rice Mochi

You can make mochi from brown glutinous rice. I've also used a combination of half white and half brown mochi rice, which is similar to regular mochi (which is made with white rice), but still has more fiber and nutrients from the brown rice. Make it in your mochi machine just like you would regular white rice mochi.

You might be able to find brown glutinous rice flour to use in this recipe instead of normal mochiko, but I haven't found any in my area.

Get Creative with Mochi

Add extracts, cocoa powder, and other ingredients to your mochi. Then pair the flavored mochi wrappers with complementary ice cream flavors.

For example, mint mochi with chocolate ice cream, coffee mochi with chocolate ice cream, chocolate mochi with peanut butter ice cream, or chocolate mochi with strawberry ice cream. Use your creativity and make gourmet treats that would cost you more than $3.00 apiece from an ice cream shop…if you could find them.

CHAPTER 14

Beyond the Cups: Ideas for Serving

Of course, you can always serve these frozen treats scooped into a bowl, dish or cup. You could also serve them in commercial ice cream cones. Be sure to check the list of ingredients on the package to be sure they are vegan.

I have not had luck so far in making homemade vegan ice cream cones. They are tricky to make and involve working very quickly with a hot cookie, wrapping it around a cone before it hardens in a matter of seconds.

So I've stuck to the non-edible bowl as a serving vessel for now. Perhaps someday I will return to the kitchen to attempt cone making again. (Cue dramatic music here...)

In the meantime, for variety, you can try serving a selection of flavors for dessert after a meal. Or have an ice cream buffet.

The idea is simple. Pick a handful of different flavors and set them out with toppings. You can choose to make fruit and chocolate sauces and caramels, although I have not included any recipes for these in this book.

Instead, set out a variety of fruits, nuts, and other goodies in small dishes, each with a spoon. Guests can grab a scoop of ice cream, then add the toppings of their choice. Here are some suggestions:

Chopped pieces or slices of fruits: pears, apples, pineapple, papaya, mango, peaches or nectarines, lychee, banana, orange segments, pomegranate seeds, etc.

Fresh or frozen berries: raspberries, blueberries, strawberries, marionberries, blackberries

Cherries, fresh or frozen

Chopped nuts: almonds, hazelnuts, walnuts, cashews, pecans, peanuts, pistachios, macadamias

Seeds: sesame seeds, sunflower seeds, pumpkin seeds, chia seeds

Chopped or broken pretzels

Chopped or broken hard candies

Shredded coconut, plain or toasted

Crushed cookies

Crushed potato chips or tortilla chips

Popped popcorn, lightly salted

Chopped candied ginger, orange, lemon, or grapefruit peel

Chopped dried fruits: dates, raisins, currants, figs, apricots, etc.

Chopped herbs: mint, basil, rosemary, tarragon

Chopped cocoa nibs

Ground cinnamon, nutmeg, cardamom, allspice

Black pepper

Sea salt

Cocoa powder

Balsamic vinegar

Yes, you read that list correctly. Although I haven't tried it myself, I've heard that the combination of strawberry ice cream with black pepper and fresh tarragon is divine.

And what's with the salt, pretzels, popcorn, and potato/tortilla chips? They've got the sweet-salty thing going. Nuts on ice cream is old hat--consider these an update to the wardrobe.

Besides, you're likely to pay big bucks to try salted chocolate ice cream in some shop or fancy restaurant somewhere. So do it at home instead.

Sprinkling the chips or pretzels on top means they won't get soggy like they do if you mix them in. You can try the recipe for Chocolate Pretzel Ice Cream (in Chapter 8, page 84) if you want to mix them in. A lot of testers liked it even when the pretzels were soggy.

Chocolate Lavender Ice Cream (page 91) with mochi pieces

CHAPTER 15

Troubleshooting

In an ideal world, every batch of ice cream you make would be delicious, non-fattening, and free from problems. In the real world, you may gain weight and run into some trouble. I can't help you lose weight, but I may be able to help you with problems making your ice cream.

Here are some common problems that people face when making these frozen treats, and how you might solve them if they happen to you.

PROBLEM: My ice cream does not freeze completely. I end up with only slush or semi-soft product.

TRY THIS: Make sure your freezer is set as cold as it will go. Some freezers won't chill the canister enough for you to get firm ice cream from it. If this happens to you, you will have to get used to freezing the finished product several more hours in your freezer, to allow it to firm up.

Freezers have colder and warmer areas in them. Be sure to place the canister in the coldest spot in your freezer. This is usually towards the back of the freezer, as close to the cold air inlet as possible.

Make sure your ice cream machine canister is completely frozen before you use it. It needs about 24 hours to freeze completely and be ready for use. I keep a canister in the freezer at all times, so I can make a batch whenever I feel like it.

If you try doing more than one batch at a time, the second batch will likely not freeze. You can buy a second canister to keep in your freezer, or try staggering your production to twice a day, once in the morning, and once just before bedtime. This may be enough time for your canister to re-freeze enough to do its job.

Be sure that your base mixture is completely chilled. The colder your base is when it goes into the machine, the firmer it will end up. You don't need to make the base the night before, but you should refrigerate all the ingredients you want to use, so that when you blend them the morning, day, or night you want to make ice cream, they will be cold already. Then you can proceed right to churning.

Most of the home ice cream machines will not give you rock-solid ice creams initially. You will end up with soft serve or slightly softer end product. I always recommend transferring it to an airtight container and putting it in the freezer for several more hours, to firm up. How long will depend on your freezer.

PROBLEM: After being in the freezer, my ice cream is now too hard to eat.

TRY THIS: Plan ahead and take it out about 5 to 20 minutes before you want to eat it, so it can soften up enough to be scooped and enjoyed. (This also prevents tongue burn.) How long it needs to sit will depend on how hard it was to begin with, and whether it was a sorbet, ice cream, or frozen yogurt. Different recipes melt more quickly than others.

For example, if you want to eat ice cream for dessert after lunch, take it out when you put your lunch together. It softens while you eat and is usually about the correct scoopable softness by the time you're done eating.

If you are serving one of these ice creams, sherbets or sorbets for a party, take it out when you start the main course, or halfway through it. By the time everyone has finished eating and done some chatting, there is usually a bit of a lull. That's when you ask, "Who is ready for dessert?"

The ice cream is usually perfectly scoopably soft by then. Of course, this depends on how talkative everyone is, how frozen the mixture is to begin with, how much you have, the size and shape of your container, and how hot it is in your room.

So try to keep an eye on it. That's part of your job as a host, after all--to try to serve delicious food at the right temperature, with the right texture.

Alternately, you can put the whole container in a microwave on high for a few seconds, to soften it up. How long will depend on how much you have in the container and how your microwave works.

For a one or two serving amount, try 8 to 15 seconds. For half a quart or so, try 30 seconds. For a full quart, 40 seconds to 1 minute, or even more, may be necessary. But be careful--too long in the microwave, and you end up with melted ice cream. Patience is important here.

One of our microwaves will make the outsides melt but keep the center soft. The other one will create a soft spot in the center of the ice cream. After a few times doing this, you'll figure out what works best in your situation.

PROBLEM: The finished product is grainy.

TRY THIS: Make sure the non-dairy milk you are using is smooth and creamy. Soymilks and coconut milk tend to be richer, creamier, and smoother in general than nut or rice milks.

Try switching to a different brand of the milk substitute you are using and see if that helps. Some coconut milks contain fillers that can leave a less-than-desirable end product. Again, try switching to a different brand.

Some ingredients will leave grittiness in the finished product. Guava, pear, and some other fruits and vegetables come to mind. You may want to take the extra step of straining the base through cheesecloth or a fine-mesh strainer before churning.

Lemon tends to cause some very tiny clumps, since it can react with the milk to curdle it somewhat. I haven't found a way to prevent this. Most testers don't even notice it.

Sometimes the finished product has a kind of grainy texture, and I don't know how to fix that, or even if it can be fixed. Most people don't even notice it. If you are one of those people that notice it and are bothered by it, AND if you can figure out how to fix it, please let me know, and I will spread the word to other readers. Thank you.

PROBLEM: The flavor is too bland.

TRY THIS: If the recipe contains spices, increase them slightly when you make the base the next time. See if that helps. People have varying degrees of taste, and some may love spices, while others prefer more subtle flavors. Increase the spices (or decrease them) as your taste buds dictate.

Try increasing the salt or sugar a tiny bit. When we eat something very cold, our taste buds get a little bit numb. So ice cream bases need to be sweeter than they would be if you were eating them at room temperature.

Try adding an extra 1 to 4 Tablespoons (12.5 to 50 grams) of sugar, agave (15-60 ml), or sweetener to the recipe to see if that helps. Or add another 1/8 to 1/4 teaspoon (0.5-1 ml) of salt.

The other thing that might help boost flavor is to increase the amounts of the flavoring components. So start with a stronger tea, more chocolate or cocoa powder, more fruit, more extract, etc. But go easy with your experimentation. Add a little bit at a time. Remember, you can always add more in, but you can't take it out.

PROBLEM: All the lemon zest is getting stuck in the mixing blade of the ice cream machine.

TRY THIS: Because some ice cream machine blade designs have a small area where tiny particles can get stuck, there isn't anything you can do to prevent this. However, after you've stopped churning and pulled out the mixing paddle, give the mixture a stir, to evenly distribute whatever bits of lemon zest, etc. were clumping there. Zest adds a lot of flavor, so don't eliminate it from the recipe.

PROBLEM: The ice cream is stuck to the sides of the canister and won't come out.

TRY THIS: Be sure you remove the finished ice cream immediately after you stop churning. Because the canister is very cold, the base will continue to freeze where it contacts the sides of the canister. If you remove the ice cream immediately, that won't happen.

Also, do not over-churn the mixture. Stop churning when the ice cream stops moving. It will tend to clump up around the mixing blade, because it has frozen to a soft-serve consistency. It's done.

You are more likely to have it stick to the sides if you continue to run the machine. Instead, stop it and remove the ice cream to a container, then put it in the freezer to store, or eat it.

Make sure you use a spatula that will not scratch or dent your canister. Be careful, because the metal is thin. I like a silicone spatula with a stiff, straight edge. I can really get the ice cream out of the canister easily and completely.

PROBLEM: The ice cream tastes chalky.

TRY THIS: This can happen if you don't like the flavor of the tofu (if using it) or the milk in your base. Make sure the tofu you are using is fresh. You might try a different brand of tofu, or try aseptic-boxed tofu instead of fresh.

Try changing to a different type or brand of milk. Some people dislike the flavor of soymilk, but are fine with rice milk or almond milk. Some people find the taste of rice milk too watery, so use soymilk or almond milk instead.

Or try another recipe altogether. For example, the texture and taste of the Rich Chocolate and the Chocolate (with Cocoa Powder) ice creams are quite different. Remember to take notes, so you can come up with a combination of flavors and textures that you will love, and you can make it again in the future.

If you are using coconut milk, be sure it doesn't have any gums or starches. Some brands thin down coconut milk with water, then add starches or gums to make a thicker product. But the result is a weak-tasting, horrible mixture that shouldn't even be allowed to be sold. It's disgusting.

Real coconut milk should have just coconut, water, and a preservative. If you are getting a chalky flavor and are using coconut milk, try using a different brand to see if that helps.

A Final Note

Okay, so my hope is that you will find as much enjoyment in making and eating your own vegan ice cream creations as I have and still do. And that you are encouraged to try new flavors and combinations, and to experiment yourself.

If you have any more questions or comments about anything, please contact me through one of my websites. Also, there is a possibility of a second book, with even more flavors, in the future, so if there is something you'd like to see in it, please drop me a line.

Be sure to help me spread the word, too. If you know someone who may find this book helpful, because of dietary restrictions or just because they might be interested, please let them know about it. (You can always buy them a copy for a gift--hint, hint!)

Feel free to spread the word by letting people taste your ice cream, too. I've convinced many dairy-eaters that vegan ice creams are delicious by giving them some. The flavors speak for themselves.

If you know of a store or business that is interested in selling this cookbook at their location, please have them contact me for more information.

You can reach me at these websites:

alinaspencil.com

almostveganinparadise.com

Now go out there and be the boss of your ice cream. Happy churning!

Index

Made in United States
Orlando, FL
22 May 2022

18093129R00124